EXPOUNDING THE GOSPEL AND LAW OF GOD
—Exegesis and Sermonic Development

EXPOUNDING THE GOSPEL AND LAW OF GOD
—Exegesis and Sermonic Development

The Path from Text to Sermon

Religion and Law Series, Volume Seven

George J. Gatgounis

WIPF & STOCK · Eugene, Oregon

EXPOUNDING THE GOSPEL AND LAW OF GOD—EXEGESIS AND SERMONIC DEVELOPMENT
The Path from Text to Sermon

Religion and Law Series, Volume Seven

Copyright © 2022 George J. Gatgounis. All rights reserved. Except for brief quotations in critical publications or reviews, no part of this book may be reproduced in any manner without prior written permission from the publisher. Write: Permissions, Wipf and Stock Publishers, 199 W. 8th Ave., Suite 3, Eugene, OR 97401.

Wipf & Stock
An Imprint of Wipf and Stock Publishers
199 W. 8th Ave., Suite 3
Eugene, OR 97401

www.wipfandstock.com

PAPERBACK ISBN: 978-1-7252-6135-8
HARDCOVER ISBN: 978-1-7252-6134-1
EBOOK ISBN: 978-1-7252-6136-5

VERSION NUMBER 052022

CONTENTS

THE PATH FROM TEXT TO SERMON | 1

INTRODUCTION | 3
  The Crisis in Contemporary Homiletics | 3
  The Manifestation of the Crisis in Contemporary
    Homiletics | 5
  The Current Crisis in Light of the Doctrine of Inspiration | 7
  The Current Crisis and Contemporary Epistemology | 9
  The Current Crisis and the State of Bible-Believing Christendom at Large | 10

HOW TO ACQUIRE BIBLICAL CONTENT:
THE EXEGETICAL PROCESS | 13
  What Is Exegesis? | 13
  A Working Definition of Exegesis | 14
  What Is Necessary for Exegesis? | 16
    Necessary Presupposition to an Exegetical Methodology | 16
  The Role of the Holy Spirit in the Exegetical Process | 18
  What Is the Exegetical Process? | 20
  Implications of Inductive Bible Study Methods | 20
  The Traditional Components of Exegesis and a New
    Proposal | 21
    The First Phase in the Exegetical Process | 22
    The Second Phase in the Exegetical Process | 24
    The Third Phase in the Exegetical Process | 24
    The Fourth Phase in the Exegetical Process—Enlargement | 25
    The Fifth Phase in the Exegetical Process—Application/
      Casuistry | 26

What Is the Relation Between These Phases of Exegesis? | 26
The Fivefold Exegetical Process Is True, Spiritual
  Interpretation | 28

HOW TO COMMUNICATE BIBLICAL CONTENT: THE RHETORICAL PROCESSES | 30
  How to Acquire Preaching "Points" | 31
    What Is a Preaching Point? | 31
    How Does One Know What Is and What Is Not a Good Preaching Point? | 35
  How to Apply the Rhetorical Processes | 36
    What Is Expository Preaching? | 36
  What Does "Exposition" Mean? And What Is the Difference Between Exegesis and Exposition? | 37
  Three Missing Elements in the Current Literature on Exegesis and Homiletics | 38
    The First Missing but Necessary Element in the Current Literature on Exegesis and Homiletics: Spiritual Consecration | 38
    The Second Missing but Necessary Element in the Current Literature on Exegesis and Homiletics: The Role of Context | 39
    The Third Missing but Necessary Element in the Current Literature on Exegesis and Homiletics: The Fusion of Exegesis and Homiletics | 39
  Outline of the Comprehensive Procedure | 41
    1. Consecration | 42
    2. Observation | 42
    3. Validation | 44
    4. Enlargement | 44
    5. Application/Casuistry | 45
  Conclusion: "Pulling It All Together" Into a Sermon | 46
    First Phase: Consecration | 46
      1.1 Examine One's Thoughts, Words, and Deeds in Light of Biblical Standards in Prayer | 47

Why Must One Examine Oneself for Exegesis to Begin Properly? Spiritual Presuppositions | 47
The Real Starting Point of True Exegesis | 50
1.2 Confess All Known Sin to God | 53
How Should One Confess Sin to God? | 53
What Should One Confess to God? | 54
1.3 If Necessary, Confess to and Reconcile with Others | 55
1.4 If Necessary, Make Restitution to Individuals and/or Institutions | 55
1.5 Consecrate One's Thoughts, Words, and Deeds to New "Universal" Obedience | 56
Second Step: Observation | 58
Observation in General | 58
2.1 Observe the Entire Book | 60
The Necessity of Contextual Overviews | 60
A Text, by Its Very Nature, Cannot Be Atomized | 61
The Beginning of the Observational Process Is a Book Overview | 62
2.1a Observe the entire book for its historical and cultural setting | 63
2.1b Observe the entire book, particularly for its main divisions, repetition within the divisions, and transitions between the divisions | 65
2.1c Observe the entire book, particularly the relations between paragraphs in sequence and interrelations between paragraphs out of sequence | 73
2.1d Determine the book's subject through observing what all the sections and paragraphs have in common, and the book's complement by observing what is distinct to each of the sections | 76
2.1e Consult key synthetic tools and revise the book's subject/complement, if necessary | 79
2.1f Record the fruits of the book overview with an analytical chart | 80
2.2 Observe the Entire Paragraph in the Original Language | 81

Why Study the Bible Paragraph by Paragraph? | 81
Why Study Paragraphs in the Original Language? | 81
Hebrew, Aramaic and Greek Are the Languages of Divine Choice | 82
    2.2a Analyze the paragraph | 82
    2.2b Interpret findings | 87
    2.2c Write an exegetical outline | 99
    2.2d Determine the paragraph's subject/complement | 106
    2.2g Make a list of interpretative questions on the passage, put them in logical order, and answer them by whatever technique or tool necessary, including the key exegetical commentaries | 107
Old Testament Exegetical/Expositional Commentaries (in a proposed order of exegetical usefulness): | 112
New Testament Exegetical/Expositional Commentaries (in a proposed order of exegetical usefulness: | 122
Converting an Exegetical Outline into an Expositional Outline | 127
What Is the Difference between an Exegetical Outline and an Expositional Outline? | 127
The "Converted" Exegetical Outline into a Preachable and Teachable Expositional Outline | 128
Converting an Expositional Outline into a Homiletic Outline | 129
An Example of "Converting" an Expositional Outline into a Homiletic Outline | 130
    2.3 Observe the Key Words in the Sentences | 131
    Why Do Differing Interpretations Exist? | 139
Fourth Phase: Enlargement Into Doctrine | 142
    The Analogy of Faith or Analogy of Scripture Principle | 142
    The Relation of Exegesis to the Analogy of Faith or Analogy of Scripture | 143
    "Biblical Theology" an Intermediate Step between Exegesis and Systematic Theology | 144
    The Method of Biblical Theological Research | 145
        Fourth Phase: Enlargement into Doctrine | 147

Enlargement through Verbal Parallelism | 147
Enlargement through Conceptual Parallelism | 148
Enlargement through Typology | 150
    4.3 Enlarge the Text by Consulting the Standard Biblical Theologies, Historic Confessions, and Systematic Theologies | 150
The Use of the Standard Biblical Theologies | 150
  The Key Biblical Theologies include: | 151
    Old Testament Biblical Theologies | 151
    New Testament Biblical Theologies | 151
    Biblical Theologies of the Entire Bible | 151
The Use of the Historic Confessions | 152
  The Use of the Standard Systematic Theologies | 153
    4.4 Enlarge the Text by Consulting Puritan and Reformed Commentaries | 155
    The Use of Puritan Commentaries | 155
An Abbreviated List of Recommended Puritan Commentaries | 156

FIFTH PHASE: CASUISTRY OR THE USES OF THE TEXT | 173
  What Is Casuistry? | 174
  Casuistry/Application Biblically Mandated | 174
  The Role of the Holy Spirit in Casuistry | 175
  The Goal of Casuistry | 176
  The Function of Casuistry | 176
  Tests of Casuistry | 177
  Casuistry and the Uniqueness of the Bible | 179
    5.1 Perform a Casuistic Treatment upon the Text to Determine Its Uses | 180
    5.2 Prepare one's heart through prayer, particularly (1) by determining personally to obey the text regardless of loss of convenience, prestige, or position, (2) by asking the Lord for wisdom not to apply the text beyond its limits or to strip the text's content, and (3) by asking the Lord for God-given care for those to whom the text applies. | 180

5.3 Brainstorm: List every conceivable scenario to which the text may apply. The "cases" to which the text may apply is casuistry. Then list corresponding questions about how the text would change each scenario. The changes to each case are the "uses" of the text. | 181

5.4 Verify That Each Change Would Not Violate the Analogy of Scripture | 183

5.5 Compare One's Own "Uses" with the "Uses" in the Puritan Commentaries and Add to or Refine One's List Accordingly | 183

5.6 Each "Use" Is a Preaching Point. Develop Each Preaching Point through the Rhetorical Processes | 183

BIBLIOGRAPHY | 185

THE PATH FROM TEXT TO SERMON

Christianity's history is one of a series of victories, interspersed with grief-inducing defeats that then provide opportunities for renewal, revival, and reform. Part of the reason for such a condition relates to failure of Christian churches. The ailing condition of our present-day church is largely an effect of spiritual malnutrition, and sermons that once nourished the faithful are now more of man than they are of God. *Exegesis and Sermonic Development—The Path from Text to Sermon,* by George Gatgounis, provides guidance to solving this decline. Dr. Gatgounis' purpose for his new book is to explain how to produce sermons that are true to the biblical text and may be used to purify our teachings and bring nourishment to our failing and feeble Church.

By the introductory title *Expounding the Law and Gospel of God* Dr. Gatgounis does not mean that his proposed exegetical method is the only method, but he does acknowledge that there are definite principles of exegesis and homiletics, which if followed, will yield a biblical sermon.

The exegetical and homiletic approach outlined in this book provides a comprehensive and efficient process that joins together what the pastor does in his study with what he does in the pulpit. This work is one of the very few exegetical works that includes the act of deliberate spiritual consecration as the foundational first step to preparing sermons that are spiritually fruitful. Dr. Gatgounis believes that since a full understanding of the Word derives from divine illumination, the exegetical process must first begin with communion with the Holy Spirit. While mere scholarly interpretation may feed a listener's mind, a sermon's true purpose is to provide spiritual nourishment. He believes that it is impossible to foster spiritual growth in others without first having one's own personal encounter with God.

The reader will discover that the methodology adopted in this work surpasses several exegetical guides because rather than launching directly into the biblical text with a lexicon in hand, Dr. Gatgounis' book encourages the reader to pursue exegetical analysis that begins with observation of context. Through this method, it is possible to conduct a more thorough analysis through the observation of a text's semantic sense and syntactical nuances. Additionally, by following the detailed chronological steps presented in this work, contextual observations become precise, comprehensive, and enriching.

Finally, this work is unique in that it rejects a longstanding notion that exegesis and homiletics are disparate endeavors requiring separate procedures. Instead, the new system presents exegesis and homiletics as equal and interdependent parts of the same preparatory activity, creating a more effective exegetical-homiletic process by which to produce accurate, biblically derived, and God-inspired sermons.

This work is filled with detailed lists of helps and references, as well as abundant examples and clear, accessible rhetoric. Biblically based teaching is the medicine by which the Church may be healed, and through this manual, we may have another tool to enrich Christ's Church by improving our sermons.

H. Wayne House, M.A., Th.D., J.D.
Distinguished Research Professor of Theology,
Law, and Culture
Faith Evangelical College and Seminary, Tacoma,
Washington

INTRODUCTION

THE CRISIS IN CONTEMPORARY HOMILETICS[1]

Walter Kaiser, in his seminal work *Toward an Exegetical Theology*, is correct in his assessment that the Church's strength is relative to her interpretive competence. In the words of John Albert Bengel, "When the Church is in strong health, the light of Scripture shines bright; when the Church is sick, Scripture is corroded by neglect; and thus it happens, that the outward form of Scripture and that of the Church usually seem to exhibit simultaneously either health or sickness; and as a rule the way in which Scripture is being treated is in exact correspondence with the condition of the Church."[2]

Bengel's observation is defensible biblically. In the eighth century B.C., the prophet Amos declaimed, "Behold, the days come, saith the Lord God, that I will send a famine in the land, not a famine of bread, nor a thirst for water, but of hearing the words of the Lord ... they shall run to and fro to seek the word of the Lord and shall not find it. In that day shall the fair virgins

---

1. Homiletics is the art and science of sermon preparation and delivery. Exegesis is the art and science of interpreting the original texts of Scripture.

2. John Albert Bengel, *Gnomon of the New Testament*, ed. Andrew R. Fausset, 5 vols. (Edinburgh: Clark, 1857–58), 1:7 as quoted by Walter C. Kaiser, *Toward an Exegetical Theology: Biblical Exegesis for Teaching and Preaching* (Grand Rapids: Baker, 1981), 7.

and young men faint for thirst … they shall fall, and never rise up again" (Amos 8:11–14).

Such a condition is so severe a judgment of God that Adam Clark remarks that "this is the severest of God's judgments on this side of the worm that never dieth, and the fire that is never quenched."[3] When the exposition of the Word languishes, spirituality languishes. "Garbage in, garbage out" may be a computer user's adage and "you are what you eat" a dietician's motto, but both illustrate an analogous spiritual principle: The Church's anemia is invariably a result of malnutrition.[4]

Furthermore, the current crisis in interpretation is basic to doctrinal imprecision.[5] If the root is unsound, so are the trunk and the branch. Exegetical weakness necessarily leads to doctrinal imprecision, that is, an inability to articulate the intricacies of Christian doctrine. The ability of the Church to convince others to embrace her doctrine depends heavily on her ability to articulate doctrine accurately.

Kaiser further comments on the resultant doctrinal inaccuracy: "The number of books and articles worth mentioning which provide both faithfulness to the text of Scripture and spiritual nourishment to contemporary men and women is so sparse and hidden in such remote journals or languages as to be of very little aid for our needs today."[6]

Kaiser's point is that interpretive incompetence invariably leads to doctrinal imprecision; and doctrinal imprecision invariably leads to spiritual impotence. This is an anatomy of ecclesiastical degeneration in a nutshell: little Word, little doctrine; little doctrine, little spirituality; little spirituality, little Church.

---

3. Adam Clark, *The Holy Bible with a Commentary and Critical Notes* (rep: n.d. [1824]), 689.

4. Kaiser, *Exegetical Theology*, 8.

5. George M. Landes, "Biblical Exegesis in Crisis: What Is the Exegetical Task in a Theological Context," *Union Seminary Quarterly Review* 26 (1970–71): 274.

6. Kaiser, *Exegetical Theology*, 18.

INTRODUCTION

In sum, a sad silence has settled on contemporary American evangelicalism, a silence that results from interpretive incompetence. Currently, this silence is the Church's greatest crisis. To counteract this silence is the purpose of this study.

THE MANIFESTATION OF THE CRISIS IN CONTEMPORARY HOMILETICS

The dearth of sound interpretation has many homiletic dimensions. One prominent symptom is sermons without substance. In such cases a biblical phrase, sentence, paragraph or doctrine provides a basic thought from which the preacher may weave the whole sermonic fabric. Perhaps, the basic thought may derive from the given text; however, the substance of the sermon does not.[7] The dichotomy between that which is derived from the text and that which is not confuses the hearers and forces them to cast themselves upon the mercy of the preacher's integrity, hoping what is said is true.

This is not to suggest that every point, sub-point, and sub-sub-point must derive specifically from the text as in strict expository style,[8] but the hearers must know that points from the preacher are points from the Bible (and preferably, they should also know the specific Bible passages whence these points are taken [Acts 17:11b]). A good sermon is a sermon that is clearly biblical—that is, a sermon that is clearly biblically derived. The people must know the sermon comes from God, and to know that, they must know the route the preacher took from the Bible to the sermon. Sermons with central themes *and* supporting points that are clearly biblical are those sermons most likely to be instruments of the Church's salvation, sanctification and revival; sermons without

---

7. Ibid., 18.

8. For an outline of this form of strict expository style, where all points derive directly from the text, see Charles W. Koller, *Expository Preaching Without Notes* (Grand Rapids: Baker, 1962).

substance reveal a serious lack—or even absence—of a correct interpretive process in sermonic development.

Another dimension of interpretive incompetence in the homiletic arena is "seminarianeze." This case is on the opposite extreme of the former. Whereas in the former case, biblical substance is sacrificed on the altar of illustrative material, anecdotal reminiscing, and homiletic fluff, the seminarianeze sermon contains data that is biblically derived and accurate, yet not adapted or made relevant to the needs and interests of contemporary hearers. Sometimes these homilies are a "dry, lifeless recounting of biblical episodes apparently unrelated to the present."[9] Others are mere interpretive restatements of the text in "seminarianeze." The restatements, though accurate, are communicated in a manner which few if any hearers may relate to their personal needs. As the listeners are bombarded and bewildered "with a maze of historical, philological, and critical detail," the sermon falls "lifeless in front of the listener."[10]

In this case, the knowledge of morphology, grammar, and syntax is strong; the relation to historical and cultural context is accurate; and the theology is technically correct. But the test of interpretation has not been completed at this point.[11] Correct interpretive process does not end in mere data; it must also include the application of data that is true to the text, to the ministry and needs of the people. The biblical data must inform the intellect, fire the emotions, and trigger the will.

Many preachers preach "to their people without ever getting on 'their wave length.' "[12] Part of the reason for this tragedy is the present-day institution of the "professional theologian." Unlike the Puritan era, where the "doctors" of the Church were functioning pastors, today's religious schools hire theologians to read the latest journals, lecture, and "publish or perish."

---

9. Kaiser, *Exegetical Theology*, 19.
10. Ibid.
11. Ibid., 20.
12. Donald Macleod, *Word and Sacrament: A Preface to Preaching and Worship* (Englewood Cliffs, N.J.: Prentice-Hall, 1960), 10.

INTRODUCTION

And to whom do these professional theologians usually write? Generally, they write to and for each other, and those who write on the popular level are disparaged for not "breaking new ground in scholarship." As a result, the "armchair theologues" develop their own language, designed by them and for their own exclusive use. This language, or jargon, shields their esoteric meanings from the common people. Like the gods on Mount Olympus, the upper religious academic caste communicates to, among, and for itself, unencumbered by the untrained mortals beneath them.

For instance, note the jargoneze in the following quotations. Admittedly, if the terms were defined, the language would be clear: "Let us first take the case when the fundamental syntax transforms a (non-axiologized) virtual taxonomy resulting from the application of a single proprioceptive category, for instance, the veridictory category."[13] Or: "A given taxonomy is, therefore, a set of axiologized semiotic squares in a relation of homologation with each other."[14] Some seminarians, having been exposed to such specialized linguistic terminology, in turn bewilder their hearers by using such language to demonstrate academia and religiosity.

THE CURRENT CRISIS IN LIGHT OF THE DOCTRINE OF INSPIRATION

The bewildering boredom alluded to in the case of seminarianeze is symptomatic of an erroneous view of Scripture; this view indicates doctrinal misunderstanding underlies the general weakness of interpretation that, in turn, undergirds biblical teaching and preaching. Boredom may be a far greater danger to many churches than heresy. If the preacher is consistently boring, it may be because his preaching material is boring to him. Boredom with the Scripture reveals a low view of the beauty of Scripture. God is not a boring God, and He did not design His word to be a boring—thereby imperfect—reflection of Himself. Likewise, Christ

---

13. Daniel Patte, *The Religious Dimensions of Biblical Texts* (Atlanta: Scholars, 1990), paragraph 6.211, 231.

14. Ibid., paragraph 6.323, 234.

was never boring. Consider, for instance, this remark made by his disciple, after an encounter with Christ on the road to Emmaus: "Did not our heart burn within us while He talked with us on the road, and while He opened the Scriptures to us?"

Furthermore, some preaching degenerates into a "Bible-less authoritarianism," where rules and standards are foisted upon the hearers without biblical documentation. The thinking is not: "These are God's standards, as indicated in these passages. Let me explain what God says and how He says it, and what we must do in light of these passages." Rather, the rationale is, "I am the man of God. Do what I tell you because I am who I am." Unfortunately, congregations with this type of authoritarianism come to be ruled not by God's law alone, but by God's law and the will of the local cleric. Some have described such authoritarians as "minipopes," whose polity is permanent martial law. Inadequate understanding of the Scripture as providing the man of God in the pulpit sole authority in matters of faith and practice underlies an unbiblical authoritarianism.

Another illustration of doctrinal declension in this area is how contemporary preachers handle the unity of the Bible. Often, whole sections of the Old Testament are wholly ignored: "We are the Church. That was for Israel. Therefore it is not for us" (*contra* 2 Tim. 3:16b). This thinking, while revealing an inferior Old Testament/New Testament interpretive system or hermeneutic,[15] also reveals an inferior view of the unity of the Scripture. The Bible is an organic whole, not a collection of fractured, unrelated parts, and failure to see a particular text as an interconnected link in the whole chain of Scripture often results in interpretations tangential to the real meaning of the text. One text, a tangent; two texts, a hobby; three texts is getting there; and four texts are legs of a table to set something on.

For instance, one astute preacher opened his Bible to Romans 8:23, and deduced from "waiting eagerly for our adoption" that

---

15. For a critique of the dispensational Old Testament/New Testament hermeneutic, see Curtis I. Crenshaw and Grover E. Gunn, III, *Dispensationalism Today, Yesterday, and Tomorrow* (Memphis: Footstool, 1985).

adoption is a future event. The preacher then proceeded to rail against the doctrine that we are presently adopted sons, because his text said that adoption was yet future. He ignored another relevant passage, Ephesians 1:5, which teaches that adoption is also a completed act ("in love he predestined us to be adopted as his sons").

THE CURRENT CRISIS AND CONTEMPORARY EPISTEMOLOGY

The general epistemology in the West in this post-Christian era is, at its essence, essentially a form of humanism. Humanism is the conceptual "placing of Man at the center of all things and making Him the measure of all things."[16] This interpretation of reality is, of course, violently divergent from the Christian world view that acknowledges the eternal glory of God as the center of all things, and the holiness of God as the measure of all things. Francis Schaeffer states that God is "the final reality," and the content of his Word is the straightedge by which all is measured.[17]

The natural interest of the humanist world view is contained within two collectives: the state and society.[18] Although these collectives may define the natural interest within a specific time and place, they lack a values base upon which to structure the state or society. The values of humanism are human conventions; therefore, they are, by their very nature, free and in flux.[19]

The Church's departure from moral absolutes—and the resultant epistemological vacuum—underscore the need for clarity in exegesis: because moral absolutes are written in the Scriptures, clear exegesis is required to promulgate them.

The most direct and objective means to determine universal moral law is to employ a correct interpretive process to determine

---

16. Francis Schaeffer, *A Christian Manifesto* (Westchester, Ill.: Crossway, 1984), 23.
17. Ibid., 28.
18. Ibid., 30.
19. Ibid., 30.

the Bible's meaning. Although there may be variation between the processes used to determine "scientific" facts outside the Bible versus the inscripturated facts within the Bible, there is no variance between the facts themselves, because both "worlds" have the same divine Author. As Schaeffer illumines:

> There may be a difference between the methodology by which we gain knowledge from what God tells us in the Bible and the methodology by which we gain it from scientific study, but this does not lead to a dichotomy as to the facts. In practice, it may not always be possible to correlate the two studies because of the special situation involved; yet if both studies can be adequately pursued, there will be no final conflict.[20]

Since the clearest window to moral absolutes is the Bible, a sound procedure to extract these absolutes is necessary for the philosophical, hence moral, health of contemporary society.

THE CURRENT CRISIS AND THE STATE OF BIBLE-BELIEVING CHRISTENDOM AT LARGE

Having lost its exegetical moorings, the Bible-believing world is left to flounder in flux and instability. As Leon Morris observes: "This is a very interesting and important time for evangelicals, a time when there are all kinds of new movements and new thoughts. Cross currents of various kinds are moving in the evangelical world."[21]

Meanwhile, the Bible remains undaunted, even amid such raging crosscurrents. Should the Church interconnect with her anchor, she too would not sway, but would instead hold steady. The Rock of Gibraltar cannot flit about like a leaf in the wind. Christ alone is the Church's rock-solid foundation, known through the

---

20. Francis A. Schaeffer, *The Complete Works of Francis A. Schaeffer: A Christian Worldview* (Westchester, Ill.: Crossway, 1972), 1:139.

21. Leon Morris, *Biblical Research: A Challenge to Evangelical Scholars* (Cambridge, Mass.: Tyndale, 1961), 1.

INTRODUCTION

authors of the sixty-six books of the Bible, whose record not only testifies of Christ, but is also the medium to come to Christ.

Christ's agents are the authors of both testaments, by whom He deposited truth through written prophecy (John 20:30-31; 21:24).[22] The apostles, for instance, comprise the authoritative agency Christ established for the proclamation of salvation (Acts 1:22, 26; 10:41; Heb. 2:2-4); it is through their authority the New Testament is delivered (παρέδοσαν (Luke 1:1-4); παρέδωκα (1 Cor. 15:3), once for all (ἅπαξ Jude 3), to us.

God is the same yesterday, today, and forever (Heb. 13:8)[23], and He designed the New Testament documents to be read with the Old Testament Scriptures (1 Thess. 5:27; Col. 4:16; Rev. 1:3).[24] The two Testaments comprise the two lips by which Christ speaks and provides resuscitation to His Church.

To deposit biblical truth into written form is an act of Immanuel, God coming to be with us—yet God is not only with us but also in us. Accordingly, there is a relational aspect to biblical truth,[25] in that the Bible is not only a book above all other books, but also a means of relationship; when mixed with prayer, Biblical truth not only provides for a relationship between us and Immanuel but is also the very substance of the relationship.

22. Compare the difference between 1 Tim. 4:14 and 2 Tim. 1:6. In the former text, Timothy was ordained by the hands of the elders, apparently to the office of teaching elder (1 Tim. 3:1ff.); in the latter, he received the gift of prophecy by the hands of Paul only. The apparent discrepancy is resolved by the account in Acts 8:14-17, where Philip's converts do not prophesy until they meet the apostles, who pray for them and lay hands upon them. Only then does the Spirit of prophecy fall upon them. The prophetic gifts of Mark, Luke, Jude, and perhaps the author of Hebrews were therefore conferred upon them by the apostles, who sanctioned their written prophecies to the Church. For a seminal discussion of these issues, see B.B. Warfield, *Counterfeit Miracles* (New York: C. Scribner's, 1918).

23. Jon Veenhof, "The Holy Spirit and Holy Scripture," The Interpretation of Scripture Today (submitted to the RES Theological Conference, Chicago 1984), PAGE.

24. H. Ridderbos, *Helisgeschiedenis en Heilge Schrift von het Nieuwe Testament. Hef gezag von het Hieuwe Testament* (Kampen, The Netherlands: J.H. Kok, 1955) as cited by Veenhof, "Holy Spirit and Holy Scripture," 4-5.

25. Ibid., 5.

Biblical truth is not only God with us, but also *pro nobis*, "God for us."[26] When the scriptures are silenced from within the Church, the Church becomes deaf to God. If she does not hear Him, she cannot follow, and other forces begin to lead her. This power vacuum may be filled by the world, in which case the Word and the world would share authority over her, or it may be occupied by preacher-tyrants who establish themselves as "minipopes" over the Church. In either event, when those who claim to preach Christ's authoritative truth, in fact, do not, their credibility falters; their lack of spiritual leadership, in turn, causes the Church to falter, in that she is unable to rally around the uncertain sound.

One of the Hebrew terms for truth, *emet*, invites "trust in its future verification." (i.e., coming events only confirm its reliability). For this reason, trustworthy men are called "men of truth." A vine is *emet* if it brings forth its expected fruit; failure to receive fruit from the plant is disappointing and disillusioning. Analogously, if the Church approaches her pulpits, and if upon stretching forth her hand to pluck spiritual fruit, she finds that fruit sickly (or if she finds no fruit at all), she hunkers down in the pain of malnourishment—that is, a curse of disappointment, disillusionment and demoralization, and even of depression and death.[27]

How can the trumpet of truth sound in the Church again? Where does sound interpretive procedure begin and how can it be implemented? A sound interpretive procedure begins with a sound definition of "exegesis."

---

26. Ibid., 6.

27. H. von Soden, "Was Ist Wahrhiet?" in *Urchristentum und Geschichte* (Tubingen: Mohr, 1951), I, 1–24, especially 9.

HOW TO ACQUIRE BIBLICAL CONTENT
The Exegetical Process

WHAT IS EXEGESIS?

The solution to the problem of interpretive incompetence lies both in the interpreter and in the interpretive procedure—that is, in both the person and the process. While, ultimately, the development of the Christian interpreter is the sovereign pleasure of the Almighty, the development of the interpreter and the formulation of an interpretative procedure is nonetheless the responsibility of the Church (2 Tim. 2:2). In *Toward an Exegetical Theology*, Kaiser challenges the Church's failed responsibility.

Although Kaiser's work seeks to remedy the need for a comprehensive route from text to sermon, his contribution is more of a procedural philosophy than a detailed manual. Exegesis is a theory and also a skill, and it may only be learned by doing; interpretation is a science and also an art, and it involves practice for mastery. If this practice is undertaken according to a sound methodology, skills will develop all the more rapidly. Therefore, beginning interpreters especially may profit from a manual that leads them by hand through a sound methodology.

EXPOUNDING THE GOSPEL AND LAW OF GOD

A WORKING DEFINITION OF EXEGESIS

A sound interpretative methodology, encapsulated in a manual, begins with a correct definition of exegesis. A map to follow from the interpretation of a text of Scripture to its proclamation begins with correct presuppositions—because correct processes have correct beginnings.

Exegesis has been variously defined. Etymologically, the term is a simple transliteration of the Greek preposition εκ (meaning "out" or "out of") conjoined with the verb ηγεομαι. This compound word's verb-component, ηγεομαι, has two semantic categories, possessing essential, core meanings of "lead or guide" and "think, consider and regard," respectively. The sense "lead or guide" applies in contexts of military commanders leading armies (*cf.* 1 Macc. 9:30; 2 Macc. 14:16), and of religious leaders leading religious bodies (Heb. 13:7, 17, 24).[1] The sense "think, consider and regard" applies in scenarios where options are considered, valued, and then sorted (*cf.* Phil. 2:3; 1 Tim. 1:12). Paul, for instance, "considered" all things "loss for the excellency of the knowledge of Christ Jesus," his Lord, having sorted out all other values as subordinate (Phil. 3:8).

Exegesis means to "lead out" and to "think out of." It is the process by which the interpreter draws out the objective concepts from within the written text and then transposes them into the context of modern life. In sum, exegesis is to lead out of the text what is in the text. Exegesis occurs when the interpreter's conceptual patterns mirror the text's own conceptual patterns,[2] with the result that the interpreter "thinks the thinking" in the text.[3]

---

1. W.F. Arndt and F.W. Gingrich, eds., *A Greek English Lexicon of the New Testament and other Early Christian Literature*, fourth edition (Chicago: University of Chicago Press, 1957), 344.

2. Ibid.

3. William Douglas Chamberlain defines exegesis similarly: "Exegesis, then, is the leading out of thoughts that the writer had as he penned a given document." *An Exegetical Grammar of the Greek New Testament* (Grand Rapids: Baker, 1987), 1.

HOW TO ACQUIRE BIBLICAL CONTENT

Exegesis is a scientific and artful application of true hermeneutical principles to the text of the original language, with a view to comprehension and communication of the author's intended meaning, and with a further view to application to life today.[4]

First, exegesis is a science. A science, by definition, is a study concerned with observed facts, systematically classified. Methods of observation must be objective and inductive.[5] The scientific aspect of exegesis, therefore, is the orderly, objective, and inductive accumulation of data contained in the text.

Second, exegesis is an art. The artful aspect of exegesis may be accurately termed its skillful aspect. Skill in exegesis is "a power of discrimination,"[6] a practical ability to know what to observe and in what order. This implies orderly reasoning and a logical approach.[7] Exegesis becomes an art when the exegete develops a "knack" on how to sniff out important kernels of meaning and to avoid unprofitable tangents.

Third, exegesis is the application of true hermeneutic principles. Hermeneutics (literally, Greek for "translate") is the general term for a philosophy of exegesis.[8] Hermeneutics is the general philosophy of how to approach the text; exegesis is work one performs in regard to a particular passage. Hermeneutics is the corpus of interpretative principles the exegete conceived before the process; exegesis begins when the exegete has started exploring a text. Hermeneutics is strategy; exegesis is tactics. Hermeneutics is

---

4. C.K. Barret, in his *Gospel According to St. John, An Introduction With Commentary and Notes on the Greek Text* (London: SPCK, 1958) states that εξεγησατο in John 1:14 means, "explain, rehearse the facts, recount a narrative." And, it is "often used for the publishing and explaining of divine secrets"; John D. Grassmick, *Principles and Practice of Greek Exegesis: A Classroom Manual* (Dallas: Dallas Theological Seminary, 1974).

5. Grassmick, *Principles and Practice of Greek Exegesis*, 5.

6. *The Oxford Universal Dictionary* (Oxford: Oxford at the Clarendon Press, 1933), 1806.

7. Ibid., 1906; *Webster's New Twentieth Century Dictionary of the English Language* (United States of America: William Collins, 1979), 1701.

8. For a helpful overview of hermeneutics, see Grant R. Osborne, *The Hermeneutical Spiral: A Comprehensive Introduction to Biblical Interpretation* (Downer's Grove: InterVarsity Press, 2006).

theory; exegesis is practice. Exegesis, therefore, must be guided by sound principles of hermeneutics.

Although Scripture includes a wide variety of genres, with each genre requiring some differing hermeneutic principles, there is one overarching principle that includes all others: Although no text has a single magic door one may open to penetrate its meaning, the most valuable aid to determining a text's meaning is to examine its context. When viewed without the light of its literary-historical-cultural context, a text becomes merely pretext. Just as some animals act very differently when they are taken out of one cage and put into another, the text outside of its context is no longer the text. Accordingly, in all theological controversy regarding the meaning of a text, the ultimate court of appeal is in its context. Francois Bovon and Gregoire Rouiller agree: "In spite of its inner coherence and its own functioning, an isolated text must be associated with other realities, that is, reinserted into diverse contexts: language, history, and consciousness."[9] Bonds exist between the text and history, language, and the way people currently think. Sound exegesis explores each bond.

WHAT IS NECESSARY FOR EXEGESIS?

Necessary Presupposition to an Exegetical Methodology

Hermeneutics is a system of presuppositions that guides the procedure of exegesis, and therefore the product of exegesis. The indispensable presupposition that guides the procedure and product of exegesis is that the words recorded by the original Author, upon the original manuscripts of the sixty-six books of the Bible, are the very words of God. To deny this presupposition is to set the procedure and product of exegesis "off," because the exegete no longer seeks to shape his thinking through the text and instead seeks to shape the text by his thinking. Because exegetes who believe they

---

9. Francois Bovon and Gregoire Rouiller, *Exegesis, The Problem of Method and Exercises in Reading*, translated by Donald G. Miller (Pittsburgh: Pickwick, 1978), 1.

handle the very words of God let the text shape them, while those rejecting the truth of the text become a law unto themselves, correct exegesis can only be performed by those who understand the nature of scriptural text is inerrant, infallible, and authoritative.

What exactly is the Scripture, the object of exegesis? The Greek term *theopneustos* in 2 Timothy 3:16, usually translated "inspired," is actually better translated "exhaled."[10] The Scriptures are the breath of God exhaled—or, inscripturated. Thus, they bear some of the qualities of their Author, including majesty, holiness, truth, unity, and power.

The Westminster Larger Catechism offers the following evidence that the Scriptures are the words of God: "The Scriptures manifest themselves to be the Word of God, by their majesty and purity" (that is, their uniqueness and divergence from all forms of human corruption), "by the consent of all the parts" (the doctrinal unity of more than forty authors having written documents of various genre over a span of at least 1,500 years), "and the scope of the whole, which is to give all glory to God" (their unique content, which is Christocentric).[11]

The Scriptures are authenticated as being *theopneusto* not only by literary characteristics but also by experiential results. By their power to "convince and convert sinners," the Scriptures authenticate their inherent authority and hence their identity.[12]

Even so, to convince a person that the Scriptures are the Word of God is ultimately the work of the Holy Spirit (John 14:6). Through His testimony, the exegete does not merely entertain a high probability of biblical truth, but instead knows with utter certainty that the Bible is truth (John 17:17).

Practically, a right understanding of the doctrine of inspiration will motivate an exegete. The realization that the words of the original autographa are the very words of God fuels a desire to

---

10. B.B. Warfield, *Revelation and Inspiration* (Grand Rapids: Baker, 1981), 77–80.

11. *The Westminster Standards. The Larger Catechism* (Philadelphia: Great Commission Publications, n.d.), 35. WCF 1:7.

12. Ibid., 35.

know what they mean. In contradistinction, if the original text is merely the work of religious visionaries and is not normative—that is, if it is not both descriptive and prescriptive of God's will—why then should it be revered? Therefore, inspiration demands a functional reverence for the words of the original text, and this functional reverence is the very fuel that powers sound exegesis.

THE ROLE OF THE HOLY SPIRIT IN THE EXEGETICAL PROCESS

Because the Holy Spirit generates a desire to know Scripture (John 14:26), some form of inductive Bible study has been the norm among historic evangelicals. The goal of such study has been to understand God's intended meaning as expressed in the biblical text.[13] To achieve this goal implies a question was posed from the outset: "How does the exegete come to know?" To this regard, Schliermacher offers the following maxims:

1) I am understanding until I encounter a contradiction or nonsense.

2) I do not understand anything that I cannot perceive and comprehend as necessary (regarding what is necessary). . . . The understanding of a particular is always conditioned by an understanding of the whole.[14]

Schliermacher, unfortunately, presupposes that the Bible may be understood as if it were any other book. Although his latter point regarding the necessity of context is accurate, the Bible is unlike any other book in content. To be sure, some common ground regarding literary composition exists between the Bible and other books, and these common literary principles may help to guide the observation of Scripture. But the actual content of the Bible,

---

13. Elliot Johnson, *Expository Hermeneutics* (Grand Rapids: Academie, 1990), 74.

14. F.D.E Schliermacher, *Hermeneutics*, ed. Keinz Kimmerle (Missoula, Mont.: Scholars, 1977), 41, 59. Italics mine.

HOW TO ACQUIRE BIBLICAL CONTENT

because it is holy, just, and good (*cf.* Rom. 7:12), is qualitatively different from mere human literature.

Uninspired literature may be perceived by the senses and comprehended by both the regenerate and unregenerate rationally. Admittedly, almost anyone can pick up the Bible, and by his senses read the text, and through his rationale comprehend the text to some degree—the doctrine of the perspicuity, or clarity, of Scripture is that the Scriptures are understandable. As the Puritan divines of the Westminster Assembly state:

> All things in Scripture are not alike plain in themselves, not alike clear unto all (2 Pet. 3:16; John 16:17; John 6:60); yet those things which are necessary to be known, believed, and observed, for salvation, are so clearly propounded and opened in some place of Scripture or other, that not only the learned, but the unlearned, in a due sense of ordinary means, may attain unto a sufficient understanding of them (Ps. 119:105, 130; Acts 17:11, 12).[15]

In a full sense, the Scripture cannot be fully understood in the same manner that one might understand conventional literature. Although the Bible contains conventional literary aspects, its content is spiritual (Rom. 7:15; 1 Cor. 2:14). Regarding the spiritual realm, Christ declaimed, "without me you can do nothing" (John 15:5). Without the Holy Spirit's illumination, there is no true spiritual comprehension of the Word. Common literary ground between the Bible and mere human literature is perceived through man's conventional wisdom; however, the spiritual dimension of Scripture may only be understood through the spiritual wisdom given by God alone (1 Cor. 2:14; James 1:5). The Author of the Word interprets the Word for the exegete through the process of exegesis, while the exegete knows what he knows because God imparts that knowledge through His agents, the Holy Spirit and the Word.

---

15. William Greene, ed. *A Harmony of the Westminster Standards* (Atlanta: John Knox, 1976), 18. WCF 1:7.

WHAT IS THE EXEGETICAL PROCESS?

What are the components of the exegetical process? What, traditionally, does it entail? Since the advent of Traina's *Methodical Bible Study*, inductive Bible study has generally been viewed as including three traditional steps: observation, interpretation and application.[16] "Induction" is the general term of logic that describes the process of reasoning from the general to the particular, and the term is commonly used for Bible study wherein the student views the text in general and draws out particular conclusions. A wide variety of Bible teachers have espoused Traina's threefold method of inductive Bible study, whereby a method is a series of steps, performed in a set order, to produce predictable results.

The first step, observation, answers the question "What do I see?" Interpretation involves learning and answers the question, "What does it mean?" Application answers both "What must I do?" and "How does it work in real life?"

The last step of application is significant, in that Bible study should always return to reality; without this last application, biblical interpretation risks becoming irrelevant, "other-worldly," and useless to the average person.

IMPLICATIONS OF INDUCTIVE BIBLE STUDY METHODS

Traina's traditional steps imply several axioms. First, this method includes both reception (through observation and interpretation) and reproduction (through application). The student receives, and then gives, what the Bible has given to them.

To reference a commonly used analogy, the Dead Sea once asked the Sea of Galilee, "Why are you so full of fish?" The Sea of Galilee replied, "If you would give as well as receive, you too would be full of life. You must give in order to grow; you will not grow until you give." There is a striking difference between a "Dead Sea"

---

16. Robert A. Traina, *Methodical Bible Study* (New York: Ganis and Harris, 1952).

student and a "Sea of Galilee" student: Both have an inlet gained through observation and interpretation, but the latter also has an outlet through application. Application that results from correct Bible-study methods helps to stem the torrent of biblical illiteracy and spiritual abnormality, in that the "method-consciousness" of the Bible student aims at self-transformation, and a commensurate confrontation of others is brought forth out of concern.

Second, the method implies that Bible study is inductive, not deductive. Too much Bible study degenerates to a regurgitation of secondary sources. Rather than to foster dependence upon Bible study tools and helps, a correct Bible study method offers a firsthand acquaintance with the text. The process is not by proxy—it is personal.

Third, as interpreters alone examine the text, they develop their own independent, analytical ability. "Pipe students" believe what is poured into them by outside sources, whereas "tree students" have their own roots in the Word. This posture, rooted in personal Bible study, develops the student's ability to evaluate critically the plethora of opinions surrounding Scripture. Moreover, the independent nature of Bible study allows the student the joy of personal discovery. The Bible is designed to excite thought, not to impede it; the Bible is not designed to bore.

Finally, the threefold approach to Bible study is not a short cut—work must be done to discover the Bible's meaning. No one will ever be an adequate interpreter of Scripture without diligence (2 Tim. 2:15). Neither is a correct Bible study method a mold—its steps are broad enough to allow for individuality, being not straightjackets but instead broad categories of discipline with which to explore the Bible.

THE TRADITIONAL COMPONENTS OF EXEGESIS AND A NEW PROPOSAL

The traditional three-step method—observation, interpretation, and application—has much merit. Its simplicity allows the beginning student to focus on three core tasks, without which no real profit in the Word can occur; however, the three-step model, entrenched as it is, could be improved.

Bible study without prayer is an exercise in carnality, if not in futility. Further, the Bible is a diverse document, not only in regard to time, place, and manner of composition, but also in its difficulty. Some passages would not challenge a small child, while others have occupied the best and brightest minds in Christendom for a lifetime. Accordingly, a focus not only on prayer but also on difficult passages could take the Bible student a step further than the traditional three-step method allows. Further, texts cannot be fully understood unless they are placed in the context of the entire Bible. The human mind, as a creation of God, naturally thinks in systems. Admittedly or not, Bible students likewise think in systems. A complete Bible study must include a focus on the way in which the student systemizes a particular passage, and effort must be made to systemize texts conscientiously, rather than with a "knee-jerk" reaction—or worse, a complete lack of consciousness and a total disregard to context.

Because its object is spiritual, the process should begin with a spiritual mindset—specifically, the spiritual discipline of prayer. Prayer is the means by which the exegete dedicates his time and text to Christ, who consecrates the time and text to the advancement of his kingdom. By the same token, prayer should end the process. Prayer is the chief exercise of faith by which we receive God's benefits.[17] The spiritual nature of the object of exegesis requires spiritual interaction with God before, during, and after the exegetical process. The more the exegetes endeavor to talk to God, the more they will hear God talk through His Word. Consider, then, a first step for the exegetical process:

The First Phase in the Exegetical Process

A directed effort to pray. Consider Psalm 119:18: "Open my eyes, that I might behold wondrous things out of thy law." This is a

---

17. See Calvin's *Institutes*, Book III, Chapter 20.

directed prayer, wherein "open my eyes," precedes an effort to observe the word, "that I might behold." Note that before observation, the Psalmist seeks spiritual interaction. Why? The Psalmist understands that he cannot observe the Word unless God performs a work upon his sensibilities. Why should he even try to look at a spiritual entity without possessing spiritual eyes? The real genesis of a spiritual exegetical process occurs before the exegete has looked at the text—the exegete must first connect with God. When the exegete and God are "on line," the information will flow, because the circuit is complete. By the genesis of prayer, exegetes look for a person in the text—Christ—whom they can feel, know, and love. The text becomes not merely cold lifeless data; God designed the Scripture to be a window to Christ, not merely religious subject matter. The Holy Spirit must "bear witness with the spirit" of the exegete (*cf.* Rom. 8:26), thereby convicting him of sin, righteousness, and judgment (John 16:8)[18]—of sin, because sin separates him from Christ, of righteousness, because this is what he needs from Christ, and of judgment, because he must understand that Christ is judged for all his sins. The transaction of spiritual business cannot occur unless the exegete intentionally, knowingly, and decidedly endeavors to pray, in the Spirit, to Christ.

About what should exegetes pray to Christ? Whatever they need. They need illumination (light being the metaphor for understanding in Scripture; *cf.* 1 John 1). They need clarity of thought, powers of observation, and desire to know. They need a hunger, a thirst, and passion for the passage. They need a clean mind brought about by repenting of that which grieves (Eph. 4:30) and quenches the Spirit (1 Thess. 5:19), thereby cleaning out the dirt to make room for the treasure. They need a mindset that grasps Christ, but lets go of self—a mind to absorb Christ and to be drained of everything else. They need to be pliable by the text, but inflexible in his loyalty to the text. And when do exegetes know that they have prayed enough to begin observing Scripture? There is no set

---

18. Admittedly, the immediate referent of this text is adoption, where the Spirit testifies in the inner man that adoption has occurred. But analogously, the Spirit is involved in illumination.

formula with which to provide an answer to this question, because the answer exists through a relationship, that is, the interrelation that takes place between the exegete's heart of hearts and the heart of God.

The Second Phase in the Exegetical Process

Observation of the books, sections, paragraphs, sentences, and words of Scripture (*cf.* Matt. 12:3; 19:4; 21:16; 22:31, "Have ye never read?"). Good exegetes see more in Scripture than do poor ones; good exegetes see Scripture more accurately than do poor ones. When poor exegetes encounter an inevitable blindness to the text, they must find some other source for the sermon's substance. The difference between the fabricator and expositor is the answer to the question, "to see or not to see?" Observation is viewing the text from every angle, from the outside in. Observation is work.

The Third Phase in the Exegetical Process

Validation is the resolution of possible explanations of a text—different explanations of meanings of words (lexical), meanings of words in relation to other words (syntactical), meanings of sentences (propositional), and doctrinal meanings (biblical-theological). Validation proceeds on the assumption that in order for a point to be authoritative, it must be true; through validation, one makes the informed determination of which meaning is true. As observation unlocks the details of the text, the text's intricacies must then be explained. Since a variety of explanations may be possible, but only one is correct, the correct view must be validated. To be sure, the meaning may include various facets or dimensions. Even so, the meaning of Scripture is "not manifold, but one."[19]

---

19. Greene, ed., *A Harmony of the Westminster Standards*, 17. WCF 1:9. "The infallible rule of interpretation of Scripture, is the Scripture itself; and therefore, when there is a question about the true and full sense of any Scripture (which is not manifold, but one), it may be searched and known by other places that speak more clearly" (Matt. 4:5–7; 12:1–7).

How are interpretive options resolved, and how does the interpreter know which one is true? Consider Acts 17:11: "For they searched the Scripture daily, to see if those things were so," and also consider the words of Jesus: "go and learn what this meaneth . . ." (Matt. 9:13). Christians often differ in their interpretations and explanations of texts. Because the Bible is an infinite book, interpretations are legion. But validation is a sound procedure to determine which interpretation is correct and true.

The Fourth Phase in the Exegetical Process—Enlargement

Enlargement of the text into doctrine (cf. Rom. 12:6: "If any man prophesy, let him prophesy according to the analogy (αναλογια) of the faith"). Before a particular Scripture can be applied, it must be set into the context of its various related texts. Each text of Scripture is a representative of a number of conceptually similar texts. These similar texts should be consulted so they may "inform" the original text. Every text has a circle of meaning, but related texts shed light on what is contained within that circle of its meaning. As related texts illumine the originating text, the originating text may also illumine the related texts. Enlargement involves looking at the text from the inside out, with the understanding that every text is an open door into a mini-theological system of related texts.

In Romans 12:6, the term "analogy" (αναλογια) is used in relation to prophesying. The term "ana" literally means "up"; "logy" refers to "words." Literally, the related words of Scripture are to be built up into an inclusive system that provides a finer and fuller focus on the meaning of the originating text. Furthermore, this system provides a foundation for application of the doctrine of which the particular text is a part. This procedure of enlarging texts according to their analogy of faith is essential for sound application, because the related texts provide checks and balances upon any conclusions the preacher may draw from the originating text.

The Fifth Phase in the Exegetical Process—Application/Casuistry

Application to every relevant case is casuistry (James 1:22, "But be ye doers of the word, not hearers only"). Casuistry is the application of the text to every case to which it is relevant. The full import of a passage may never be apprehended until it is applied to life. In order to fully believe the text, one must behave according to the text. To understand the creed contained in the text, one must conduct one's life according to the content of the text.

Application exports content out of the world of the Bible and into the world at large. It puts the truth to work; it is truth transforming what it touches.

Scholarly treatments of the application element of the exegetical procedure are rare. The mood in contemporary scholarship is the "we are not called to apply anything; we are called to sit around and talk about the Bible. Our role is to impress other Bible-believing, and hopefully liberal, scholars." The aura in such scholarly circles is that of minds in flux: the mass of differing interpretations "float" around in minds, but rarely are the lines drawn between truth and error—thi swould be "too dogmatic." On theological differences, it is *avant-garde* to be piously agnostic, never to commit to anything because one is "balanced" and "open-minded." In contrast, true exegesis occurs when the exegete has a mind to commit wholly to truth, to expound what is right and expose what is wrong. True exegesis produces belief that behaves. Exegesis that simply fuels the interchange of ideas that never leave the cranium produces Christians whose creeds and conduct are וָבֹהוּ תֹהוּ, *tohu va bohu* (Hebrew for "without form and void").

WHAT IS THE RELATION BETWEEN THESE PHASES OF EXEGESIS?

These phases relate to each other in a cumulative fashion. Each builds upon the other. They are links upon a chain; and a chain, of course, is only as strong as its weakest link. Consecration opens the door of the heart for truth to enter. Observation ushers in the truth. Validation clarifies what the truth means. Enlargement explores the truth in its fullest dimensions. Casuistry applies the truth to every conceivable scenario.

Because application of truth is bound to expose sin, the last phase of the process leads the exegete to re-consecrate. Sin is a barrier between the exegete and the Bible. When the exegete responds to such exposure, consecration is initiated. Therefore, application leads to consecration. Consecration sets the stage for the exegete to assimilate new truth. Once new truth is observed, possible explanations for what is observed are validated. Upon validation of what is observed, enlargement allows an individual truth to be placed in the context of related truth. Through such expansion, tangents from an individual text are thwarted, and peripheral truths regulate and balance the central truth. When the individual truth is perceived in such a context, a wider focus allows for more intelligent application. The exegete then perceives that it is not a mere fragment of truth to be applied, but the whole "mini-system" of doctrine of which the text is a part. Upon application, sin is further exposed; repentance in the consecration process takes place, and the exegetical wheel continues to turn.

The turning of the exegetical "wheel" results in significant benefits. First, if the exegetical "wheel" continues to turn, the exegete is more and more dying to sin and living to righteousness. The exegete is becoming more holy, more righteous, and more Christ-like. The exegete is learning how the truths he observes fit in his own overalls; thus, he is learning how truth affects life, not only his own life but also the lives of others.

Secondly, through the enlargement phase, the exegete is formulating and building sound and systematic doctrine, so that he does not observe, validate or apply Scripture in a vacuum, but rather sees truth as a system. His approach to Scripture is not atomized; instead, he is continually being introduced to related texts, thus gaining a much better grasp of the Bible.

Thirdly, the exegete is continually repenting of his sins. John Calvin remarked that even the most saintly man is aware only of ten percent of his own sins. The repeating cycle awakens the exegete to his own sins in the application phase, while the consecration phase includes repentance and renewal to obedience. Continual repentance provokes humility. Humility promotes dependence upon the Spirit for illumination. Illumination from the Spirit prompts keen observation. Thus, the circular process promotes the development of men and women of God.

Fourthly, the Holy Spirit is therefore active in this repeating cycle. He is not left out of the process, but actively takes part because the procedure directly involves Him.

Finally, the validation phase forces the exegete to check and re-examine what he sees. If the observation process generates conflicting explanations, he must then rigorously compare differing views in order to arrive at the correct one. The enlargement phase further requires him to check what he has validated.

In sum, the repeating cycle is organic and total. It is organic, in that it lives rather than degenerates into a lifeless transference of data from a book to the cerebrum; it is total in the sense that it involves and engages the whole person. Because the whole person is engaged, involving the will, emotions, and affections, rather than merely filling the mind with dead (inorganic) thoughts and bare-boned facts, the whole person may provide a whole message. As Ralph Waldo Emerson remarks, "what you are stands over you the while, and thunders so that I cannot hear what you say …"[20] A mind may reach a mind; a heart may reach a heart. But a whole person can change a whole person. The true exegetical cycle produces a holistic communicator.

THE FIVEFOLD EXEGETICAL PROCESS IS TRUE, SPIRITUAL INTERPRETATION

As the Father seeks ones to worship and serve Him "in spirit and in truth" (John 4:23), true Spirit-wrought interpretation involves each element of the five-fold cycle. Real interpretation includes

---

20. Ralph Waldo Emerson, "Social Aims," 1875.

HOW TO ACQUIRE BIBLICAL CONTENT

the illumination of the Spirit, which requires: (1) consecration; (2) thorough observations, correctly explained; (3) validation of correct explanations; (4) consultation of the analogy of Scripture, or enlargement; and (5) application. Interpretation that includes all five elements is the path to preachable, teachable, and usable content; it is the spiritual means to the desired spiritual end.

HOW TO COMMUNICATE BIBLICAL CONTENT

The Rhetorical Processes

The solution to the current crisis in homiletics is twofold. On the one hand, content or substance is lacking: the people need "stuff to chew on." "Exegesis" is the means by which to acquire biblical content for effective preaching. On the other hand, communication and rhetorical clarity are lacking: the people need to understand. "Rhetoric" is the way to say things in order to be understood. Rhetoric is the means to communicate points clearly. A "point" is simply a complete idea expressed in a sentence.

There are five rhetorical ways to communicate a point:

1. Explanation provides understanding. Explanation answers the question, "what does it mean?"

2. Argumentation provides acceptance of an explanation. Argumentation adopts a debate mode, and it answers the question, "should I buy it?" (or, "is it true?").

3. Illustration provides visualization of an explanation. Illustration is a pictorial mode, and it answers the hearers' question, "what does it look like?"

4. Exhortation provides motivation to believe and to behave in accordance with the text. Exhortation is a "coaching" mode, and it answers the question, "would you encourage me

through this?" (The preacher's exhortative response communicates, "let's do it!")

5. Application provides concerned confrontation and a challenge to change. Application mode is the "brass tacks," "nitty-gritty," "rubber meets the road" mode; it is truth "in overalls." Application answers the questions, "how can I do this in real life?" and "how can I change?"

HOW TO ACQUIRE PREACHING "POINTS"

What Is a Preaching Point?

Preaching (or "homiletic") textbooks typically refer to preaching points as "propositions." Similarly, George Frederic Seiler's classic work on hermeneutics, or the science of biblical interpretation, describes how such preaching points are derived from the Bible:

> The natural order of ideas in each proposition is accordingly fixed by the form of the laws of human thoughts. Hence, then, the rule: in every proposition first seek the subject, then the predicate, afterwards the copula, and point out the relation in which the former stands to each other.[1]

This passage underscores a law of human thought and language: Complete ideas are communicated through complete sentences, and sentences are composed of subjects and verbs; therefore, valid preaching points are sentences characterized by possessing subjects that are biblically derived and justified, verbs that are biblically derived and justified, wherein the relation between the two is biblically derived and justified.

Haddon Robinson describes how subject-predicates comprise the central preaching point of a whole sermon.

---

1. George Frederic Seiler, *Biblical Hermeneutics Or the Art of Scripture Interpretation* (London: F. Westley and A.H. Davis, 1835), 14.

When we talk about the subject of an idea, we mean the complete, definite answer to the question, "What am I talking about?" The term subject is being used in a technical sense. For example, the subject as it is used in homiletics is not the same thing as a subject in grammar. A grammatical subject is often a single word. The subject of a sermon idea can never be only one word since it calls for the precise, full answer to the question, "What am I talking about?"[2]

Furthermore, it is important to add that for preaching and teaching to be biblical and effective, hearers that attend to the words of the preacher or teacher should ask, "What is he talking about?" And they should readily see that the answer to that inquiry and the answer to the question, "What is the text talking about?" is one and the same.

Robinson's statement refers to the subject of a whole sermon and therefore to a whole text; however, his subject-principle applies to the text as a whole as well as to all its parts, since all texts of any conceivable scope have subjects:

1. The Bible, wherein "Christ" is the subject [*cf.* Luke 24:27]

2. A whole testament (for example, the subject of the Old Testament, about which Gerhard Hasel says that no single concept can cover all of the "bases," since its subject is "God himself")

3. All the writings of related biblical authors (for example, Moses and Joshua both discuss the establishment of Israel as a nation in their land [*cf.* Josh. 1:1–5]; the Old Testament prophets command Israel to "obey or be destroyed" [*cf.* Jer. 12:17])

4. All the writings of a single biblical author (for example, Moses' great subject is "Yahweh's holiness imposed upon his people" [*cf.* Lev. 19:2]; Paul's great subject is "the work of Christ in the New Covenant Church" [*cf.* Rom. 16:25–26])

2. Haddon W. Robinson, *Handbook to Biblical Preaching* (Grand Rapids: Baker, 1980), p. 39; *cf.* p. 41. The expository preacher "pursues the subject and complement when he studies the Bible. Since each paragraph, section, or subsection of Scripture contains an idea, an exegete does not understand a passage until he can state its subject and complement exactly."

5. A whole book (for example, Genesis describes "the sovereignty and providence of God" [Gen. 1:1]; Exodus is "to know God" [Exod. 6:3])

6. A section within a book (for example, Romans 1–3, "all have sinned")

7. A paragraph (for example, Luke 1:1–4, "Luke's purpose in writing his Gospel")

8. A sentence (for example, Rom. 12:1–2, "presentation of one's life for service")

9. A word (for example, "righteousness" in Rom. 3:25)

10. A grammatical form of a word (for example, the singular form of "seed" in Galatians 3:16)

Robinson expands the subject/predicate relationship further, to include a subject/complement relationship, as well.

A subject cannot stand alone. By itself it is incomplete, and therefore it needs a complement. The complement "completes" the subject by answering the question, "What am I saying about what I am talking about?" A subject without a complement dangles as an open-ended phrase. Complements without subjects resemble automobile parts not attached to a car. An idea emerges only when the complement is joined to a definite subject.[3]

A complete idea—or "point—is a complete sentence, consisting of both a subject and a complement. Consider again the previous list of "macro-" to "micro-" texts, now with complements attached to each of the subjects:

1. *The Bible* ("Christ saves his elect people" [*cf.* Luke 24:46–49; Matt. 1:21])

2. *A whole testament* ("God himself, through the New Covenant, saves his elect people" [*cf.* Heb. 13:20–21])

3. *All the writings of related biblical authors* (for example, Moses and Joshua, "The establishment of Israel as a nation in their land includes divinely instituted morals, ceremonies,

---

3. Ibid., 40.

civil law, and military conquest [*cf.* Exod. 3; Exod. 6; Deut. 34:9–12; Josh. 1:2–9]; Old Testament prophets, "Obey or be destroyed because your covenant God is holy" [*cf.* Jer. 12:17])

4. All the writings of a single biblical author (for example, Moses, "Yahweh's holiness is imposed upon his people through regulations on their whole lives—tribal order, travel, sacrifices, diet, jurisprudence, and family relations" [*cf.* Lev. 19:2]; Paul, "the work of Christ in the New Covenant Church effects personal salvation, Jew-Gentile equality and unity, and godly living [*cf.* Eph. 2:11–22])

5. A whole book (for example, Genesis is "the sovereignty and providence of God supervises the development of his people" [Gen. 12:1–3]; Exodus is "knowing God, which means leaving sin's slavery to worship him freely" [Ex. 6:1–8])

6. A section within a book (for example, Romans 1–3, "All have sinned because the extent of sin includes pagan, Jew, and moralist")

7. A paragraph (for example, Luke 1:1–4, "Luke's purpose in writing his Gospel is to present the matters concerning Christ")

8. A sentence (for example, Rom. 12:1–2, "Presentation of one's life for service is both logical and the will of God")

9. Words within sentences (for example, "Righteousness is imputed by God" in Rom. 3:25)

A preaching point is a complete thought composed of both a subject and a complement, both biblically derived and biblically related to each other.[4] When a text is chosen, be it a "macrotext" or one typical in size (for example, ten to twelve verses in the Old Testament, or one to three verses in the New Testament), the whole text has a subject/complement, as does each and every division within that text. The subject/complement of the whole text is the subject/complement of the sermons, while the subject/

---

4. Robinson defines an idea as "a distillation of life that abstracts out of the particulars of experience what they have in common and relates them to each other." Ibid., 45.

complements of the parts of the text are the points that support the central subject/complement of the sermon.

Jay Adams refers to these points with the term *telos* (τελοι, singular *telos*, τελος).[5] The term *telos* denotes not only the text's meaning but also its intended purpose for its audience. Adams emphasizes that a preaching point is the text's message, to be heralded by the preacher to the people.

The subject/complement relationship is two-dimensional, requiring various observations of the texts—and it is also the most efficient method of piecing together points, or *teloi*. When a student of Scripture undergoes the process of determining the subject and complement, the student must ask questions and analyze. Such analysis results in a better grip and grasp of the Scripture's content.

The first such observation for the subject asks, what is the text talking about? or, what circle does the text draw around itself? or, what parts of the text limit it, (i.e., define its scope)? The complement requires a second observation, and it is charged with answering, what does the text say about what is in the circle? or, what parts of the text interpret its defining or limiting part—that is, what part of the text interprets the subject? What the text adds to its subject is its complement.

Adams' concept of the *telos*, though valuable in that it emphasizes that points must be relevant to present-day hearers, lacks the depth of the subject/complement approach, and therefore its high potential for accuracy.

How Does One Know What Is and What Is Not a Good Preaching Point?

A good preaching point meets three criteria:

1. It is a complete sentence, composed of language that is both understandable and relevant to its particular audience.

---

5. Jay Adams, *Preaching with Purpose* (Grand Rapids, Mich.: Baker, 1982), 23ff.

2. Its subject accurately conveys the limiting, defining, and summarizing aspects of its text.

3. Its complement accurately conveys the supplemental, or "adding," aspects of the text. In short, a *good* preaching point is a *biblical* preaching point, expressed in language that is understandable to a particular audience.

HOW TO APPLY THE RHETORICAL PROCESSES

Martin Lloyd-Jones states in *Preaching and Preachers*, "Preachers are born, not made."[6] To preach effectively is to possess an ability that only the Holy Spirit can supply, that no method can supply and no amount of practice can supply. The ability to apply the rhetorical processes to preaching points, therefore, simply requires a "knack" for it. If this "knack" is there, it can be improved upon with practice; but again, either it is there from the start, or it is not.

What Is Expository Preaching?

Preaching is traditionally divided into three categories: topical, textual, and expository. In topical preaching, the central thesis is derived from the text, main points are derived from other texts, and sub-points are derived from still other texts. In textual preaching, the central thesis and the main points are derived from the text, and the sub-points are derived from other texts. In expository preaching, however, the central thesis, main points, and sub-points are derived from a single text. Although the threefold manner of delineating sermons according to structure is helpful, it is also limited in that all true preaching is expository. If the sermon's thesis comes from a particular text, but its main points come from other texts, the main points then must accurately exposit the other texts, and not necessarily the text by which the sermon's thesis originates.

---

6. D. Martyn Lloyd-Jones, *Preaching and Preachers* (Grand Rapids: Zondervan, 1971), 119.

WHAT DOES "EXPOSITION" MEAN? AND WHAT IS THE DIFFERENCE BETWEEN EXEGESIS AND EXPOSITION?

Exposition is second-generation exegesis. Exegesis is what one does in the study; exposition is what one does in the pulpit. The exegesis of a passage is time bound; its findings include facts relevant to the particular author, surrounding history, cultural milieu, and particular recipients. For instance, in the command to "walk the extra mile" (Matt. 5:41), exegesis identifies the local Roman law that required Jews to carry a Roman soldier's armor for a mile; therefore, the exegetical subject/complement might be "walk the extra mile as per Roman law willingly."

The exposition of this passage should honor the relevant facts about its cultural and historical setting. But since truth is eternal and universal, exposition goes beyond the time in which it was written and adapts the particular material to a present-day audience. The expositional point to a present-day audience might be "fulfill at least the minimum requirements of all civil laws willingly." This point contains the "kernel" in the exegetical point but adapts the point's timeless truth to the needs of a contemporary audience.

Since expository preaching points are exegetical subject/complements adapted into timeless truths, who then is actually doing the proclaiming? If the points are expositional, the one who proclaims is the Holy Spirit, through the minister of the Word. Understanding that the personality and character of the minister obviously plays a role, what does the Spirit proclaim? If the preaching is expositional, the Spirit Himself proclaims the Word.

Expository preaching, therefore, is the proclamation of the Holy Spirit, in the language of the hearers, consisting of biblical points composed of subjects and complements, all biblically derived from exegesis and expressed rhetorically.

THREE MISSING ELEMENTS IN THE CURRENT LITERATURE ON EXEGESIS AND HOMILETICS

Three elements are absolutely essential to the processes of exegesis and homiletics, yet they are lacking in the plethora of books written on the subjects. This study attempts to counteract these areas of marginal or nonexistent development.

The First Missing but Necessary Element in the Current Literature on Exegesis and Homiletics: Spiritual Consecration

First, virtually none of the many exegetical and homiletic books already written include the necessity of spiritual consecration before beginning sermon preparation. Apparently, this is thought "beneath us" or "something for the snake-handlers" or "pietistic." But could one commit a heinous crime, then immediately plunge into the most holy writings of God, and then accurately receive God's message? Will God illumine sin-darkened hearts?[7]

The Bible repeatedly warns against those who approach the Bible without consecrated hearts (Lev. 11:44; 20:7). Disregard of this warning is one of the reasons preaching lacks biblical content. The Bible is a sharp scalpel that probes the inner recesses of the heart. If the heart of the preacher is not washed with "Betadine," so to speak, it may become infected. A heart full of debris is not ready to house the treasures of God (2 Cor. 6:14; 7:1).

Therefore, it is biblically imperative that the heart be spiritually prepared—consecrated—for the process to be spiritually fruitful. Admittedly, a "head" having received the Word may reach the "heads" of the congregation—but only a life can reach a life. The preacher cannot truly probe the Bible any more than the Bible has probed him.

---

7. Ironically, like Balaam, one could. The long-term effects, however, of persistence in sin will hamper interpretation. In Balaam's case, God eventually terminated his life (Num. 22–23; 31:8).

The Second Missing but Necessary Element in the Current Literature on Exegesis and Homiletics: The Role of Context

Second, some well-known and widely used exegetical guides initiate the exegetical procedure by plunging directly into a "text." For instance, in one well-known exegetical guide, there are twelve steps, wherein step nine is examination of the context and steps seven and eight are, respectively, grammatical analysis and lexical analysis. The dreadful fallacy of the order of the steps is that every time a word is used, it is used in a new context. Some linguists even say that every word used in a new context is a new word. Because texts without contexts are pretexts, texts must be viewed from the outside in before they can be viewed from the inside out.

There is a difference between the encyclopedic sense of word (containing all its possible nuances) and its semantic sense (its sense in a particular sentence). It is impossible to determine the semantic sense of a word without a thorough grasp of the context. Furthermore, grammatical forms may be correctly determined without context, but how the forms are used in a sentence or paragraph—that is, their syntactical nuances—also cannot be determined without regard to the context.

Thus, the observation of any text of any size must begin with the context, and because the Holy Spirit divided His literary work into sixty-six self-contained wholes (or units), the logical beginning of contextual observation is the book context. Texts cannot be "atomized," and the book in which a text appears provides the basic chemistry to analyze every "atom" within it.

The Third Missing but Necessary Element in the Current Literature on Exegesis and Homiletics: The Fusion of Exegesis and Homiletics

Third, virtually all available homiletic and exegetical guides imply that first there is the exegetical process, and then it ends—with a ten-foot reinforced concrete wall, so to speak—demarcating its exegetical end and marking the beginning of the homiletic process.

This demarcation of the exegetical and homiletic processes is faulty. Instead, the two phases should be intertwined, because the two "feed" upon one another: When an exegetical point appears to the preacher, the preacher pauses to prepare to communicate that particular point; the preacher then exegetes again to acquire another point, and then pauses again to prepare to communicate. In this manner, the preacher moves from content acquisition through exegesis, directly to communication preparation through rhetoric. This dual mode is a far more efficient approach to exegetical-homiletic procedure than preparation through two separate and distinct phases of preparation—exegesis only, then homiletics only.

To illustrate, seminary or Bible-college students may enter an academic building to a first-floor classroom to learn Greek, or Hebrew and Aramaic. They may go down the hall to learn exegesis in a classroom sixty feet away. Then, they may proceed to another classroom on the third floor of the same building and be told, "preach us a sermon in front of the video camera." The students may do well in Greek and Hebrew, and even exegesis, but they may leave what they learned on the first floor when they go to the third floor. Why should they start from scratch in the homiletics classroom? The students suffer from academic compartmentalization lacking integration of all the skills necessary for biblical preaching. Good preaching requires an interweaving of a variety of skills. The process of text to sermon, therefore, should interweave the skills to sew the fabric of good sermonic material.

Since content and communication are the two legs upon which the preacher walks, to employ one without the other would cause the preacher to hop about, and probably fall. Therefore, in an effort to heal this rampant spiritual lameness, this study attempts to outline a procedure that involves the discovery of exegetically based points and how to communicate them, through a cycle of five phases: consecration, observation, validation, enlargement, and casuistry.

OUTLINE OF THE COMPREHENSIVE PROCEDURE

This procedure is a repeating living cycle. It is not a dead, mechanical application of the scientific method to Scripture; instead, the proposed outlined method involves people. Particularly, it engages the soul, seeking to wed exegesis with personal piety.

The following is an outline of a procedure that is both exegetical and homiletic. Note that the first step is preparatory and functions in the sphere of the relationship between the exegete and God. Steps two, three, four, and five consider possible preaching points, since good sermons are constructed from good preaching points, logically arranged.

The relation between application and consecration is most significant. Good application begins in one's own life, and upon application of Scripture to the exegete's own life, the exegete may need to reconsecrate his life. Hence, the exegete is ripe to repeat step one of the procedure. Reconsecration allows the exegete to begin the procedure again with a new passage. In other words, good exegesis involves the life of the exegete. Divorcing exegesis from the growth of the soul is a monumental tragedy. This tragedy, however, is commonplace.

Each repetition of this fivefold cycle should yield deeper and deeper consecration. Deeper consecration better prepares the exegete to observe, validate, enlarge, and apply Scripture. Consequently, the whole of the exegete's life will improve with each repetition of the cycle. Each repetition of the fivefold cycle should transform the exegete to greater Christlikeness. Accordingly, true exegesis is not intellectual but holistic; not abstract but personal; not dead but alive.[8]

---

8. For comparison, the reader may compare the outline of Gordon Fee, *NT Exegesis: A Handbook for Students and Pastors* (Philadelphia: Westminster, 1983), 15-20, Walter L. Liefield's excellent *NT Exposition* (Grand Rapids: Zondervan, 1984), William J. Larkin's *Manual of Greek Exegesis for Preachers* (n.p.: W.J. Larkin, 1987), and the OT exegetical procedure of Douglas Stuart, *OT Exegesis: A Primer for Students and Pastors* (Philadelphia: Westminster, 1980), 19-22. These works are the most significant contributions in the field of exegetical method applied to homiletics. (2) Comparison of Fee's, Liefield's, Larkin's, and Stuart's methods with this method may reveal relative strengths

1. Consecration

   1.1 Examine one's thoughts, words, and deeds in light of biblical standards in prayer.

   1.2 Confess all known sin to God.

   1.3 If necessary, confess to and reconcile with others.

   1.4 If necessary, make restitution to individuals and/or institutions.

   1.5 Consecrate one's thoughts, words, and deeds to new "universal" holiness.

2. Observation

   2.1 Observe the entire book.

       2.1a Observe the entire book for its historical and cultural setting.

       2.1b Observe the entire book for its main divisions, repetition within the divisions, and transitions between the divisions.

       2.1c Observe the entire book for relations between paragraphs in sequence and interrelations between paragraphs out of sequence.

       2.1d Determine the book's subject through observing what all the sections and paragraphs have in common, and the book's complement by observing what is distinct to each of the sections.

       2.1e Consult key synthetic tools and revise the book's subject/complement, if necessary.

       2.1f Record the fruits of the book overview with an analytical chart.

---

and weakness in each method. (3) Further, the reader may wish to develop their own outline of exegesis and sermonic development utilizing any part of any of the methods listed.

2.1g Formulate preaching points and apply the rhetorical processes.

2.2 Observe the entire paragraph in the original language.

    2.2a Analyze the paragraph.

        (1) Form a mechanical layout that delineates phrases, clauses, sentences, and logical relations between sentences.

        (2) Form a structural layout that identifies deep structure.

        (3) Form a grammatical diagram.

    2.2b Interpret findings.

        (1) Interpret all syntactical relationships.

        (2) Interpret figures of speech, using the grammatical diagram.

    2.2c Write an exegetical outline.

    2.2d Determine the paragraph's subject/complement.

    2.2e Make an ordered list of interpretative questions, and answer them by whatever techniques or tools necessary, including the key exegetical commentaries.

    2.2f Formulate preaching points and apply the rhetorical processes.

2.3 Observe the key words in the sentences.

    2.3a Determine which words require a full word study, in light of:

        (1) the book's subject/complement

        (2) the paragraph's subject/complement

        (3) the book's historical and cultural background

        (4) theological controversy

2.3b Follow procedures for OT/NT word studies.

    (1) Follow procedure for an OT word study.

        (a) OT full word study

        (b) OT "mini" word study

    (2) Follow procedure for a NT word study.

        (a) NT full word study

        (b) NT "mini" word study

2.3c Formulate preaching points and apply the rhetorical processes.

3. Validation

   3.1 Validate rival interpretative options.

   3.2 Isolate the nature of the validation—textual, lexical, syntactical, stylistic, biblical-theological, and/or systematic-doctrinal.

   3.3 List the options, including exegetical evidence for and against each.

   3.4 Make an exegetical decision.

   3.5 In light of the solved validation problem, formulate preaching points and apply the rhetorical processes.

4. Enlargement

   4.1 Enlarge the text into doctrine, using the whole of Scripture.

   4.2 Enlarge the text through verbal parallelism, conceptual parallelism, and typological parallelism.

   4.3 Enlarge the text by consulting the standard biblical theologies, historic confessions, and systematic theologies.

   4.4 Enlarge the text by consulting Puritan and Reformed commentaries.

4.5 Formulate preaching points and apply the rhetorical processes.

5. Application/Casuistry

5.1 Perform a casuistic treatment upon the text to determine its uses.

5.2 Prepare one's heart through prayer.

    5.2a Determine personally to obey the text regardless of loss of convenience, prestige, or position.

    5.2b Ask the Lord for wisdom not to apply the text beyond its limits or to strip the text's content.

    5.2c Ask the Lord for God-given care for those to whom the text applies.

5.3 Brainstorm.

    5.3a List every conceivable scenario to which the text may apply. These scenarios are casuistry.

    5.3b List corresponding questions about how the text would change each scenario. These changes to each scenario are the *uses* of the text.

5.4 Verify that each change would not violate the analogy of Scripture.

5.5 Compare one's own uses with the uses in the Puritan commentaries. Add to or refine one's list accordingly.

5.6 Each "use" is a preaching point. Develop each preaching point through the rhetorical processes.

Conclusion: "Pulling It All Together" Into a Sermon

    A. Take the homiletic outline developed in 2.2e and pray over each point.

        1. Pray over the text's thesis first.

        2. Pray over the text's preaching points next.

    B. Weave the preaching points taken from other steps into the homiletic outline.

    C. Develop the preaching points.

        1. Seek illustrations for preaching points; answer "What does this point look like?"

        2. Develop explanations for preaching points; answer "What does this point mean?"

        3. Devise arguments for preaching points; answer "Why should I believe or obey this point?"

        4. Draw up exhortations for preaching points; answer "What encouragements are there for me to believe or obey this point?"

        5. Use applications of preaching points; answer "How will this point change my life and the lives of others?"

    D. Organize the sermon into a final draft.

    E. Rehearse the sermon as many times as necessary.

    F. "Preach the Word!" (2 Tim. 4:2).

First Phase: Consecration

Consecration is essential to initiate, perform, and apply exegesis. Only a right relationship to the Spirit is a fructifying relationship with the Spirit.[9] Sin separating the exegete from God and inhibit-

---

9. Jon Veenhof, "The Holy Spirit and Holy Scripture," *The Interpretation*

ing the Spirit's fruit bearing must be confessed and forsaken. The Holy Spirit is not only the source of the message but also the very life (Rom. 8:10) of the messenger; He is not only the source of written inspiration (*cf.* 2 Sam. 23:2) but also the source of ability to perceive it (*cf.* 1 Kings 22:24; Isa. 30:1; 48:16; 61:1; Zech. 7:12; Neh. 9:30; 1 Chron. 12:18; 2 Chron. 15:1; 20:14; 24:20).[10]

Because the exegete is a fellow worker (συνεργῳ; 1 Cor. 3:9) with the Spirit, the exegete must be in a consecrated state. The effort to exegete is not 50 percent divine and 50 percent human; it is 100 percent divine and 100 percent human.[11] When the interpreters fully consecrate themselves, they are in the condition to offer the full 100 percent spiritual effort to interpret.

The exegete and the Spirit, according to Veenhof, become a "communing council," whereby the Spirit illumines, witnesses, comforts, and admonishes the exegete. But the illumination, witness, comfort, and admonition by the Spirit is objective. The Spirit will not and cannot illumine, witness, comfort, or admonish, except according to the objective standard of the text itself and the whole of Scripture. Thus guided by the Spirit, the exegete not only knows but also experiences the meaning of Scripture, so that he can say authoritatively, "Thus saith the Lord."[12]

1.1 EXAMINE ONE'S THOUGHTS, WORDS, AND DEEDS IN LIGHT OF BIBLICAL STANDARDS IN PRAYER

Why Must One Examine Oneself for Exegesis to Begin Properly? Spiritual Presuppositions

The method to explore the Bible's contents must reflect the reality that the subject matter is not human but divine. The process delineated in later steps of this procedure may be effective in interpreting

---

of Scripture Today (submitted to the RES Theological Conference, Chicago, 1984), p. 13.

10. Ibid., 3.
11. Ibid., 9–10.
12. Ibid., 14.

any literature, be it of literary note (Plato, Shakespeare, Dante, Milton) or of religious note (*Tale of Aquat, Bhagavad Gita, Talmud, Koran*)—but because the spiritual literature to be analyzed in Holy Scripture is unlike any other, the spiritual condition of the interpreter is crucial.

The designation "holy" literally means "distinct" from everything else, including anything within its class. The Bible is unique in its spirituality as a result of: (1) its author, the Holy Spirit; (2) its content, which includes the only revealed way of salvation; (3) its end, which is to give all glory to God; and (4) its own self-definition, that it is holy (2 Tim. 3:15).

The unique spirituality of the Bible demands a spiritual approach on the part of the interpreter.

It Is Human Nature to See What One Wants to See

The Spiritual Condition of the Exegete Influences Their Perception of the Scriptures

The principle that it is human nature to see what one wants to see is observable from both positive and negative perspectives. Negatively, sinful inclinations of the heart distort and dim perception. Eliab, for instance, angrily rebukes David, because he perceives David's inquiries as an evidence of pride (1 Sam. 17:28). But in reality, David's inquiries about the giant's blasphemies are motivated by concern not for himself but for his God (1 Sam. 17:32ff.). Eliab's passivity in the face of such blasphemy evidences greater concern for his safety than for God's glory. This character flaw distorts Eliab's perception of David's true motivation.

The princes of Ephraim provide another negative illustration of the same principle. Envy causes the princes to perceive Jephthah's "group of adventurers" (which excludes them) as a threatening enemy that is worthy of extermination, when in reality they were allies (Judges 11:3; 12:1–6). Jealousy twists their perception of a friend into that of an enemy (Judges 12:1).

Likewise, because Joab was covetous of Abner's higher position (2 Sam. 3:26–39), Joab similarly saw Abner not as an ally but as an enemy to exterminate. Covetousness twists perception. Sin debilitates perception.

Achan, Simon Magus, and Ananias and Saphira each also demonstrate the relative blindness produced by covetousness. Achan's materialism blinded him to the reality of God's all-seeing eye; because he was blind to God's presence with His people, he thought God would be blind toward his theft of the Babylonian garment. Covetousness likewise distorted Achan's ability to perceive reality.

Simon the Sorcerer was similarly blinded (Acts 8:9–24), perceiving the Holy Spirit not as a gift to enable him to overcome sin but as a tool to gain supernatural power. Ananias and Saphira saw a lie as a means of gaining prestige in the Church at Jerusalem (Acts 5:1–11), rather than as a direct offense against the Holy Spirit.

Each of these allusions demonstrates that sin distorts human judgment. Sin dims the perception of the potential exegete; character flaws may twist his perception of spiritual realities. Because the interpretive process is, essentially, perception of a text, the interpreter's heart condition is crucial to the process. Humans tend to perceive according to their nature; therefore, our nature must be as objective as possible. Because sin destroys objectivity, spiritual consecration should initiate the interpretative processes.

Other biblical allusions confirm the positive potential of this principle. The extremities of Joseph's positions as a favored son (Gen. 37:1–39:20), persecuted sufferer (39:21–41:36), and supreme sovereign (41:37–50:26) illustrate that a right heart condition sharpens perception. Because of his inward condition, he perceives his normal role and responsibilities as steward for his father. Although unjustly incarcerated twice, Joseph's inward attitude causes him to see his prisons not as occasions for bitterness but as opportunities for service, in that his inward condition determines how he perceives the work of Providence. The manner in which Joseph's inner character shapes his outer perception is illustrated not only through adversity but also prosperity, in that he does not view his newly acquired power as an instrument of revenge against his brothers; his inner motives shape positively his outer perception of God's works.

In a similar vein, David's heart condition shapes his perception of Goliath's insults. While his colleagues perceive Goliath's insults to be justification for their passivity, David perceives the insults directed at his God as reasons to be active (1 Sam. 17:32ff.). David's consecration allows him to see through the morass of self-deception, into reality. A right heart condition sharpens spiritual insight.

The Real Starting Point of True Exegesis

The Profits Derived from the Exegetical Process Are Dispensed by God Alone

If tangential and erroneous interpretations are to be avoided, many factors in the exegetical process must be correct; however, the first matter that must be "correct" is the heart of the interpreter. Good exegesis does not begin in the text but in the heart of the one who aspires to unlock the text's true meaning.

In exegesis, the "revealing" is executed not by the interpretive process but by God Himself—Revelation occurs not *by* the method but *through* the method, because the source of understanding is not the interpretive process but instead God himself. An interpretative procedure is only a conduit through which God may illumine.

Some procedures may be better than others; like channels of water that may allow water to pass more rapidly and in greater volume than would an inferior channel, the water nonetheless originates outside the channel itself. Similarly, the light that comes to the interpreter comes from the Father of lights, and the exegetical process should be the most clear, effective lens with which to magnify that light.

When Peter received the illumination that Jesus was the Messiah (Matt. 16:13–19), God was the source: "This was not revealed to you by man, but by my Father in heaven." The conversation with

Jesus and the disciples was only the channel through which God revealed this truth to Peter. Similarly, God also was the source of all the various revelations before Christ was born on earth (Heb. 1:1). Both Paul and John confirm that God sovereignly dispenses spiritual understanding: Christ is the light that enlightens mankind (John 1:4, 9), to the point that Christians do not necessarily need any human teacher (1 John 2:27). Paul agrees that the Spirit is the source of revelation, and that revelation comes not by man, nor by the works of man (1 Cor. 2:10). Because the source of spiritual insight is God Himself, the focus of the interpretative process is not mechanical but spiritual. The focus is not on the method but on the Master. Exegesis is a spiritual conduit whereby God imparts spiritual understanding to the soul.

A Warning to the Exegete: The Bible Has Potential to Harden as Well as to Bless

Exposure to the contents of the Bible does not necessitate character transformation (*cf.* Rom. 12:2). To the contrary, the Bible may be an instrument of judgment to harden the heart of the interpreter. The Tannaic scribes were required to memorize the entire Old Testament, and Pharisees had extensive exposure to the Scriptures, yet wove consistent and far-reaching patterns of hypocrisy. "Beware the leaven of the Pharisees" (Matt. 16:6), who "going about to establish their own righteousness, did not submit themselves to the righteousness of God" (Rom. 10:3). Their selective obedience was a cloak with which to cover their real character, a character Christ describes as "dead men's bones and everything unclean" (Matt. 23:27). The pattern of the scribes and Pharisees therefore underscores that character transformation is not an inevitable result of exposure to the Bible. Furthermore, their exposure to God's revelation, as it was revealed through the words and miracles of Christ, resulted in obduracy: they stupidly denied the healing of the man born blind (John 9:26–34) and paid Roman sentries to lie about the resurrection (Matt. 28:11–15). Exposure to God's revelation may result in greater hardening.

Truth may aggravate the evils of human nature just as well as it may liberate human nature from its evils (*cf.* John 8:32). The unique spiritual nature of the Bible may be an instrument God uses to harden the proud, and at the same time, it is a conduit God employs to apply grace to the humble (*cf.* Prov. 3:34; James 4:6). Humility demands that one see God as He truly is and to see man as he truly is. A humble state of heart is the result of the Spirit's work (Gal. 5:22–23), through the instrumentality of consecration (*cf.* James 4:10); God promises to make His dwelling with the humble (Isa. 57:15).

The Exegetical Process Should Be a Means for the Exegete to Depart from Sin and Approach God

The exegetical process is a means to comprehend not a concept but a Person. Interpretation does not merely acquire data but also enhances a relationship with a personal God; the interpreter is to be a disciple, not a data processor. The goal of the exegete is to know God, not merely facts about God.

Scripture distinguishes the mere knowledge of facts about God from the personal experience of God. Six times in the book of Exodus, God explains that His reason for delivering His people is so that they may know Him (6:7; 7:17; 10:2; 16:12; 29:46; 31:13). The Hebrew term "know" (ידע) does not signify a mere intellectual assent or comprehension, but rather a knowledge born of personal experience, as evidenced by the term's use in the following contexts: physical relations (Gen. 4:1, 17), childlessness (Isa. 47:8), sickness (Isa. 43:4), and punishment (Jer. 16:21).[13]

Exodus outlines the way one may experience God. To experience God is to escape the slavery of sin: The vocabulary of deliverance—*leave, get out, go out, go up, depart, delivered*—describes the extraction from sin. The taskmasters, Pharaoh, his army, and the toil of captivity picture the painfulness and detention of sin. The Red Sea miracle, the theophany at Sinai, and the

---

13. For a fuller treatment, see Rudolph Bultmann, "γινωσκω," *Theological Dictionary of the New Testament*, ed. Gerhard Kittel, trans. and ed. by Geoffrey W. Bromiley, 10 vols. (Grand Rapids: Eerdmans, 1964), 1: 696–701.

tabernacle worship portray the communion of God's people with God, whereby this communion is actually a spiritual union with God, or, a new nearness and closeness to God. They experience spiritual union with God by sight (they saw God's works), and by sound (by night and by day they could listen to the sound of God's thundering at Mount Sinai).

Similarly, the exegetical process should be a means whereby the exegete departs from sin and personally communes with God. The goal of exegesis is spiritual union with God. It is not a mere intellectual expansion, but an integral part of the Christian's spiritual pilgrimage. In the book of Exodus, the physical journey of God's people pictures their spiritual pilgrimage. The experience of God, therefore, involves progression and movement out of sin's control, and forward and upward to meet God. The exegete must never forget that his first responsibility is to approach God as a disciple and a Christian.

Furthermore, in the book of Exodus, the experience of God involves conflict—Exodus 1: midwives versus pharaoh; Exodus 2: Moses and Israel versus Egypt; Exodus 3–4: Moses versus God; Exodus 5–15: God versus Pharaoh; Exodus 16–19: the people versus God; Exodus 32–34: the people versus God. These conflicts demonstrate that the experience of God involves the perpetual struggle between sin and righteousness. In exegesis, the exegete's depraved nature is bound to conflict with the contents of his study; therefore, exegesis should be viewed as a means of the exegete's sanctification from indwelling sin and his transformation into the image of Christ (2 Cor. 3:18). Real, spiritual, exegesis transforms one's totality, not merely one's mentality.

1.2 Confess All Known Sin to God

How Should One Confess Sin to God?

In Matthew 6:12, our Lord commanded His people to petition as follows: "Forgive us our debts, as we forgive our debtors." To pray such is to ask "God, for Christ's sake, to freely pardon all our sins" (*cf.* Psalm 6, Psalm 32, and Psalm 51 with Rom. 3:24, 25).[14]

The following attitudes characterize confession: (1) acknowledgment that we are "guilty both of original and actual sin, and thereby we are debtors" to the God of justice (Matt. 18:24; Rom. 5:19); (2) further acknowledgment that "neither we nor any creature can make the least satisfaction" to God "for that debt" (Rom. 3:9, 19; Ps. 130:3; Micah 6, 7).[15] The actual prayer of confession for ourselves is that God, through His free grace, "through the obedience and satisfaction of Christ (understood) and applied by faith, would acquit us from the guilt and punishment of sin" (Rom. 5:19; Rom. 3:24, 25; Acts 13:39).[16] The term "forgive" means literally "release from a debt." The acquittal that one seeks in confession is release from the penalty of sin, so that God may act not as Prosecutor and Judge, but as Defendant and Friend.

What Should One Confess to God?

What one must confess to God is, of course, sin. But how does one come to know what is sin? "Sin is the transgression of the law" (1 John 3:4). The law in Scripture, therefore, is the means to expose the sin. "I had not known sin, but by the law" (Rom. 7:7). The law is the means whereby the exegete may examine his heart and ascertain his present spiritual condition. God's law is summarily comprehended in the Ten Commandments, and these commandments remain the perfect rule of righteousness (James 1:25; 2:8, 10; Rom. 3:19). Too often, because modern evangelicals fail to see these commandments as a summary of the whole duty that God requires of man in both Testaments, they dismiss them as irrelevant and useless. The Ten Commandments, if understood, are of great use to the exegete as he prepares to read the Scriptures; the moral law is a searchlight upon the multitude of one's sins, and it

---

14. James Benjamin Green, ed., *A Harmony of the Westminster Standards.* Shorter Catechism, Question 105. (Atlanta: John Knox, 1976), 70.

15. Ibid., 70.

16. Ibid.

exposes how much one is in need of Christ, for "his fulfilling it" and "enduring the curse" of it (Rom. 3:20; 6:14; 7:4, 5; 8:1, 3, 34; 2 Cor. 5:21; Gal. 3:13, 14).

Questions 98–152 of the Westminster Larger Catechism present an outstanding English language exposition of the Ten Commandments in the English language. The exegete, working through each of the questions, and comparing each commandment with the plethora of related Scriptures in the catechism footnotes, may allow the light of God's moral law to penetrate and expose his heart. "By the law is the knowledge of sin" (Rom. 3:19–20). Sin in general, and sins in particular, compose the barrier between man and God; to know one's sins is the first step to dealing with them, thereby removing the barrier.

1.3 If Necessary, Confess to and Reconcile with Others

Real exegesis should be an act of worship that enhances all relationships; therefore the exegete should correct, therefore, social offenses. Matt. 5:23, 24 reads: "therefore, if you bring your gift to the altar, and there remember that your brother has anything against you, leave there your gift before the altar, and go your way; first be reconciled to your brother, and then come and offer your gift."

1.4 If Necessary, Make Restitution to Individuals and/or Institutions

If others have been in any way harmed materially or financially, the general equity of Old Testament passages on stealing requires restitution (Exod. 22:1–4). Give back or pay back what has been taken. If one needs forgiveness from anyone, one must seek and acquire it. The exegete's conscience must be clear.

1.5 Consecrate One's Thoughts, Words, and Deeds to New "Universal" Obedience

Purity of heart is a necessity to correctly understand the Scriptures: "blessed are the pure in heart, for they shall see God" (Matt. 5:8). "If ye love me keep my commandments" (John 14:15). "If anyone will do my will, he shall know of the doctrine" (John 7:17). If the heart of the exegete is unwilling to obey fully, the exegetical process will build Jerusalem with "wood, hay, and stubble" (1 Cor. 3:11–14), and her walls with untempered mortar (*cf.* Ezek. 13:10–12).

Baxter, in his *Practical Directory*, outlines the following steps of preparation to reading the Scripture. Of the ten steps he provides, eight are elements of spiritual consecration:

I. Bring not an evil heart of unbelief.

II. Remember that it is the very law of God which you must live by, and be judged by at the last.

III. Remember that it is the will and testament of your Lord, and the covenant of most full and gracious promises.

IV. Remember that it is a doctrine of unseen things, and of the greatest mysteries; and therefore come not to it with arrogance as a judge.

V. Remember that it is a universal law and doctrine, written for the most ignorant as well as for the curious.

VI. Bring not a carnal mind, which savoreth only fleshly things, and is enslaved to those sins which the Scripture doth condemn; "The carnal mind is enmity with God" (Rom. 7:7, 8).

VII. Compare one place of Scripture with another, and expound the darkest by the help of the plainest, and the fewer expressions by the more frequent and ordinary, and the doubtfuler points by those which are most certain; and not on the contrary.

VIII. Presume not on the strength of your own understanding but humbly pray to God for light; and before and after you read the Scripture, pray earnestly that the Spirit which did indite it, may expound it to you, and keep you from unbelief and error, and lead you into the truth.[17]

To expand further, Puritan divines of the Westminster Assembly prescribed the following maxims for the spiritual reading of Scripture, stating that the holy Scriptures are to be read:

(1) with an high and reverent esteem of them (Ps. 119:97; Neh. 8:5; Isa. 66:2);

(2) with a firm persuasion that they are the very word of God (1 Thess. 2:13; 2 Pet. 1:16–21);

(3) and that only he can enable us to understand them (Ps. 119:18; Luke 24:44–48);

(4) with desire to know, believe, and obey, the will of God revealed in them (James 1:21, 22; 1 Pet. 2:2; Mark 4:20);

(5) with diligence (Acts 17:11; Deut. 11:13);

(6) and attention to the matter and scope of them (Acts 8:30, 34; Matt. 13:23);

(7) with meditation (Ps. 1:2; 119:97);

(8) application (Acts 2:38, 39; 2 Sam. 12:7; 2 Chron. 34:21);

(9) self-denial (Gal. 1:15; Prov. 3:5);

(10) and prayer (Ps. 119:18; Luke 24:45).[18]

---

17. Richard Baxter, *The Practical Works of Richard Baxter* (Ligonier, Pa.: Soli Deo Gloria, 1990), p. 477. Note that the first eight of Baxter's 10 points of preparation for the reading of the Scripture are spiritual in nature. The final two are:
Read some of the best annotations or expositors.
When you are stalled by any difficulty which overmatcheth you, note it down, and propound it to your pastor, and crave his help (if the minister of that place be ignorant and unable) or go to some one that God hath furnished for such work. Ibid., 478.

18. Green, *Harmony of the Westminster Standards*. Larger Catechism, Question 194, 18.

The first four of the quoted elements deal with consecration; elements five, six and seven involve observation and interpretation; elements eight and nine involve application. Most importantly, the latter element, prayer, should permeate each and every phase of the exegetical and homiletic processes. The exegete should pray to consecrate; pray as he observes and observe as he prays; pray as he interprets and interpret as he prays; pray as he enlarges the text and enlarge the text as he prays; and pray as he applies and apply as he prays. The extraction of homiletic points likewise should be commingled with prayer. The exegete/homilist that would have lasting spiritual impact must "pray without ceasing" (1 Thess. 5:17) if the power of the Lord is to be present in his ministry (*cf.* Mark 1:35–39).

A covenantal renewal should precede exegesis, wherein the exegete makes peace with God through confession, repentance, and a vow to new obedience. The goal in sanctification was, according to the Puritans, "universal holiness": "then shall I not be ashamed, when I have respect unto all thy commandments" (Ps. 119:80). Unless the exegete is in a spiritual condition to read, observe, and obey the Scriptures in this manner, he proceeds to build a house on the sand (Luke 6:46–49).

SECOND STEP: OBSERVATION

Observation in General

What Does It Mean to Observe Scripture?

How does one read with a mindset to observe Scripture? The reason some interpreters are superior to others is that they see more—more facts, in more detail and with greater objectivity. They simply read better. Eleven times in the Gospels, the question is asked, "Have ye never read?" (*cf.* Matt. 12:3; 19:4; 21:16; 22:31; Mark 2:25; 12:10; Luke 6:3).

A variety of present cultural influences discourage the development of the ability to read. The average high-school student, for instance, will spend more time watching television than listening to class lectures. The vocational trend, where education is viewed merely as a means to get a job rather than to broaden intellectual horizons, also tends to underestimate the importance of the art of reading.

Frankly, if Christians became better readers, they might once again become society's leaders. The course of Christian history could be changed beyond recognition, if Christians learned to read better and faster. To read—and read correctly—is to strengthen that tool which receives the truth.

An excellent introduction to the art of reading, including how to peruse a book, come to terms with the author, determine the message, and read various academic disciplines, is Mortimer J. Adler's *How to Read a Book*. The mind is a muscle, and reading is its exercise. To read and to read correctly is to strengthen that tool which receives the truth.

Since written revelation presupposes that those to whom the revelation is given know how to read, it is imperative that the interpreter read efficiently.

The following list of general guidelines may improve reading efficiency:

[1] *Read with a Socratic mindset.* Ask questions such as, "What is the author's intended meaning?" "How does he develop his argument?" and "What are his key terms and what do they mean?" and "What are the exegetical obscurities that must be clarified?" A spirit of inquiry and an active mind are necessities for the interpreter (*cf.* Prov. 2:1ff., where the seeker of wisdom must seek it as if it were gold). The interpreter's overall skill may be evaluated by his ability to ask the right interpretive questions, in the right order.

[2] *Read with a prayerful mindset.* Before Bible study, pray for illumination. During Bible study, pray for illumination. After Bible study, pray for illumination. In general, the Bible student must be a prayer warrior, consistently offering supplications for personal consecration, thoroughness in observation, accuracy in interpretation, and proper application.

[3] *Read with a persistent mindset.* The average interpreter quits when obscurities or difficulties appear, and many blessings are lost at the greatest point of discovery. Furthermore, persistence in Bible study prompts repetition, and the real meaning of a passage will oftentimes dawn on a interpreter after numerous readings of the text.

2.1 Observe the Entire Book

The Necessity of Contextual Overviews

What is context? Why is context important? Context is simply a perimeter, a circle around a given portion of Scripture. The size of context considered may be canonical (the whole Bible), or it may include one Testament, a genre (such as narrative, poetry, prophecy, and apocalyptic), an author's writings, a book, a discourse or section, a paragraph, or even within a single sentence. Because the book level of context is the most pronounced of contextual divisions, book context is the most logical, workable, and safe starting point for the exegetical procedure.

Several hermeneutic principles underscore the necessity of interpreting any given text in light of its immediate, broad, and historical contexts. First, the Scriptures have but one Author; therefore, what He says in one place must square with what He says in another. Second, Scripture is language, and the meaning of words is determined by the use of those words within that language. Third, Scripture defines itself. A word, phrase, clause, or sentence may have a plethora of meanings out of context, but context narrows the meaning of any Scripture segment to one meaning.[19]

---

19. Vern Poythress, 21.1 unpublished notes, "Hermeneutics," Westminster Theological Seminary, Fall/Spring 1989-90.

A Text, by Its Very Nature, Cannot Be Atomized

Because no text is complete in itself, the beginning of the observational process is not the text itself. The observational process cannot begin with the morpheme, word, phrase, clause, sentence, or even paragraph, because every text is organically bound to its surroundings., and every text is part of an author's continuous line of argumentation.

For instance, the word "board" in one context may mean a group of men, such as board of directors; in another sense, a "board" may be a piece of wood. In John 1:29, the term *world*, or *kosmos* (κοσμος), means all the nations of the world: there is only one Savior for the world. In John 12:19—"the world is gone after him"—the term "world" (κοσμος) is a hyperbole to represent the multitude following Jesus in the triumphal entry. Contextual considerations illumine the actual sense of the term *all* (πας) in Phil. 4:13. Paul does not mean that through Christ he can do anything and everything in existence, *reductio ad absurdum*—fly to the moon and back, travel through time, or split the atom. Rather, the context in verses 10–14 delineates the parameters of the "all." Whether abased or exalted, poor or rich, in adversity or prosperity, he can do all that God expects of him, because of Christ-imparted strength and despite external circumstances.

To fragment a text from its context as a matter of method virtually guarantees interpretative error. The morass of heresies that has plagued the Church for nearly 2,000 years is the mutant fruit of an atomized approach to Scripture. Johnson, in his work *Expository Hermeneutics*, articulates that the understanding of context is essentially the act of understanding itself.

> Understanding comes as I read the text. I understand what I am reading, word for word, sentence by sentence, as each new component fits "necessarily" in relation to what I understand the author to be saying in general. This understanding of what the author is saying is determined by the sense of a whole that 'conditions' the meaning of each part. Whenever I come to a word or sentence that does not fit, it means I do not really understand. It does

not fit either because it contradicts or because it is unrelated and so is nonsense—nonsense because I descry a meaning that does not fit in context with what the author says as a whole.[20]

Context is a grid. When the exegete observes the interrelationships of the part to the whole and how these interrelationships condition the meaning of the parts, then the exegete understands. Packer agrees:

> If we would understand the parts, our wisest course is to get to know the whole—or at any rate, those parts of the whole that tell us, in plain prose, the writer's central ideas. These give us keys to all his work. Once we can see the main outlines of his thought and have grasped his general point of view, we are able to see the meaning of everything else ... and how the puzzling passages fit in with the rest.[21]

The Beginning of the Observational Process Is a Book Overview[22]

With what scope of context does the process begin? The actual exegetical process begins with overall context. Contexts vary in scope from the general to specific: (1) the entirety of Scripture, (2) an entire Testament, (3) an entire group of books of similar genre (for example, the Old Testament Prophets, Old Testament Poetic Books), (4) books by related authors (for example, Mark and

---

20. Johnson, *Expository Hermeneutics*, 74–75.

21. J.I. Packer, "Biblical Authority, Hermeneutics and Inerrancy," in *Jerusalem and Athens*, ed. E.R. Geehan (Philadelphia: Presbyterian and Reformed, 1971), 144–45.

22. This is not to deny the previous phase on spiritual consecration. The beginning of the actual process in the Scriptural analysis is the whole book.

Peter[23]; Luke and Paul[24]), (5) books by one author (for example, the Pentateuch, Pauline epistles), (6) a book itself, (7) a section within a book, and (8) a paragraph.

For several reasons, the observational process should begin with an overview of the book context. (1) The most pronounced form of contextual division is the book division. The Bible is obviously divided into sixty-six contextual units, called books. The Holy Spirit clearly divided his work into these self-contained, self-completing "wholes." Each of the sixty-six books of the Bible possesses a unique internal structure. Because the content of each book is structured uniquely, any given text's interpretation depends on the book's structural thought flow.

Each book of the Bible possesses a unique controlling purpose that binds it into a coherent unit. Any particular text, therefore, exhibits a direct relation to the book's overall purpose. Although a book may have subordinate purposes, to have an additional another controlling purpose would have merited another book of the Bible. Therefore, from a pragmatic standpoint, the book is the most workable unit, and since a larger sphere is too unwieldy for a beginning, observation generally should begin at the book level. Furthermore, even if one requires a larger scope, working on one book at a time is more efficient.

2.1A OBSERVE THE ENTIRE BOOK FOR ITS HISTORICAL AND CULTURAL SETTING

All books of the Bible, under the Holy Spirit's inspiration, were written through and by humans, in human contexts, to human audiences; therefore, the "human" aspect of Scripture includes each

---

23. Mark probably drew much of his information about Christ from Peter; some New Testament interpreters see Mark's gospel as "Peter's Gospel." Compare Chester K. Lehman's discussion of the "servant of the Lord", *Theology of the New Testament* (Scottsdale, Penn.: Herald, 1974), 55ff., with Peter's sermon, Acts 2:22ff.

24. Similarly, Paul and Luke were companions (*cf.* Acts 16:12; 20:5; 2 Tim. 4:11; Col. 4:14; Phile. 24) and therefore interacted on the life of Christ and the growth of the early church.

book's surrounding history, culture, and literature of the book of the Bible. The first step in observation of a book is to develop a "feel" for this extra-biblical context.

For instance, Paul's epistles follow the standard form for a first-century Roman letter: first the writer, then the recipients, followed by a greeting, the body, and finally, the conclusion. In Deuteronomy, Moses follows the basic form of a Hittite suzerainty treaty, wherein the conqueror "lays down the law" for the conquered nation, first a historical prelude, then a list of covenant stipulations, followed by a promise of blessings and threat of curses, and finally, a charge to obedience. Ezekiel's writings follow the basic form of the *Tale of Marduk*, in that he writes of the call of the prophet by the deity, who provides the prophet a list of the sins of the deity's followers, as well as a view of the deity's dwelling place in heaven that is then described in the writing. Some Psalms follow the basic poetic pattern of Ugaritic psalms to Baal, and Ecclesiastes follows the pattern of an Akkadian autobiography. God thus delivered His own message in manners that were similar to the current literary forms of the people to whom he spoke.

In addition to its literary forms, the "human" aspect of a book includes its historical and cultural elements. In Ruth, for instance, when transactions regarding the Levirate marriage ordinance are effected between parties, a shoe is removed by the party giving the wife. In another example, Isaac's blessing imparted to Jacob, rather than to Esau, is indicative of the time and culture in which it was written, wherein the family patriarch would declare his final will and testament verbally. In relating the events of the books of Kings and Chronicles, extra-biblical knowledge regarding the kings of Assyria, Egypt, Babylon, Moab and Ammon informs of the historical settings of the various accounts of the kings of Judah and Israel. Likewise, Samuel's record of the protracted conflict with the Philistines would be illumined by a knowledge of the culture, history, military weaponry and strategy, and politics of the Philistines.

How to Determine the Historical/Cultural/Literary Setting

To orient the exegete to the background matters that surround a book, his approach must be marked by inquiry, according to the "six faithful serving men" in the old poem:

> I have six faithful serving men
> Who taught me all I know;
> Their names are What and Where and When
> And How and Why and Who.

The following standard general questions are useful in determining the essential facts that comprise a book's setting:

1. What are the major political, cultural, and economic events that provide a backdrop for the book?
2. Where was the book written, and from where does its contents transpire?
3. When was the book written, and from when does its content transpire?
4. How is the book an outflow of its author's own spiritual experience? How do experiences in his own life affect his book's content?
5. Why (or what for what the occasion) was the book written?
6. Who wrote the book? To whom is it written? About whom is it written?

2.1B OBSERVE THE ENTIRE BOOK, PARTICULARLY FOR ITS MAIN DIVISIONS, REPETITION WITHIN THE DIVISIONS, AND TRANSITIONS BETWEEN THE DIVISIONS

The Goal of a Book Overview Is Determining Its Structure

The goal of a book overview is the absorption of the book's structure. When interpreters become able to think through the book without utilizing the text, they are then ready to start analyzing individual paragraphs. It is more profitable to think through a book's structure than it is to recite the book from memory, *verbatim*, without knowing the book's meaning. Of course, memorizing a book is valuable, but the ability to think through the basic ideas of a book in its textual order is essential before beginning investigation of a single paragraph of Scripture.

To understand the goal of thinking through a book's structure, the interpreter must understand the definition of structure. Structure is merely patterns of thought that exist in the relation and interrelation of component parts. Whenever there are two textual components (discourses, paragraphs, sentences, clauses, phrases, or even individual words), there is some relation between them, and thus there is structure. Therefore, interpreters do not look solely for what God says but also for how He says it, they seek not only content but also composition, and they search not only for facts but also form.

Structure is the interrelationship and arrangement of all the book's concepts, and it is the way by which an author communicates his mind. Biblical inspiration was not dictation but allowed for stylistic freedom.[25] This measure of freedom was not separated from the Spirit's authority but instead superintended to restrain the author from error. This "elbow room" allows for the great structural diversity in the Bible. The book overview's goal is that the interpreter becomes "at home" with the book's structure.

Structure, moreover, is used not only "to convey ideas, to narrate facts, to teach, or to express feelings," but also "to give them form."[26] The meaning of a given segment of literature is "revealed fully only when every detail is grasped in relation to the form." In a sense, therefore, a particular in a given form is interpreted "in its own image, after its own likeness."[27] Regarding the common forms in a genre, the most important question is not "to what

---

25. H. Ridderbos, *Het Woord, het rijk en onze verlegenheid* (Kampen, The Netherlands: J. H. Kok, 1968), 67.

26. Meir Weiss, *The Bible From Within: The Method of Total Interpretation* (Winona Lake, Ind.: Eisenbrauns, 1984), 272. M. Steinman, Jr., "Structure," ed. Alex Preminger, *et al., Princeton Encyclopedia of Poetry and Poetics* (Princeton: Princeton University, 1974), 812–13.

27. Weiss, *The Bible from Within*, 273.

genre does it belong?" but "what is the form's unique structure?"²⁸ To illustrate:

> The "Ode on a Grecian Urn" cannot be defined by what it has in common with other odes. Even after this, and other similar aspects of it have been exhausted, what constitutes the excitement and interest of the poem will remain as intact and mysterious as before. What we are seeking is the essence of the work, what it contains that makes it the "Ode on a Grecian Urn," what constitutes its personality so to speak, a work of literature exists by virtue of what is virginal in it, what is uncontaminated and unique in its mode of being.²⁹

Some interpreters argue that the conclusion of any piece of literature is its most significant component; it is "a gesture of exit, and like all gestures it has expressive value." The manner in which it concludes becomes, in effect, "the last and frequently most significant thing it says."³⁰ In a similar vein, the Rabbinic interpreters were sensitive to conclusions. They observe in the Mishna that "we find that the prophets conclude their works with words of praise or of consolation, except Jeremiah, who concludes with words of rebuke."³¹

Other interpreters grant the primary place of significance to the conclusion but propose special attention to both the conclusion and introduction. A modern Rabbinic interpreter describes the introductions and the conclusion of the Psalter, stating that the introductions offer an "attempt at tempestuous expressions that leave a power of impression," while the conclusions "leave on a positive note."³² In the Psalms, Gunkel proposes observing first the conclusion, together with its opening for the "clearest indication

---

28. Ibid.

29. Damao Alonso, "Towards a Knowledge of Literary Works," *The Critical Moment* (London: Faber and Faber, 1964), 148.

30. B. Hernstein Smith, *Poetic Closure: A Study of How Poems End* (Chicago: University of Chicago, 1968), 196.

31. Weiss, *The Bible from Within*, 274.

32. D. Yellin, *Ketavim Nivharim* (Jerusalem: n.p., 1939), II, 12, 21.

of the genre of the Psalm." In general, the opening and closing, but particularly the closing, of a book of the Bible deserve special attention.[33]

Guidelines for Determining Book Structure

The following are guidelines for structural observations. These guidelines presuppose that there are recurring structural patterns in books.

1. *Look for Structural Focal Points.* The thought patterns of a writer often revolve around central foci; therefore, book sections revolve around such foci. These foci may include:

   a. *Central characters*—biographical foci. Genesis and Acts, for example, are structured around key personages. In Genesis, biographical foci include Adam (1–5), Noah (6–11), Abraham (12–20), Isaac (21–26), Jacob (27–36), and Joseph (37–50). In Acts, the narrative first revolves around Peter's evangelization of the Jews (1–12), then Paul's evangelization of the Gentiles (13–28).

   b. *Central locations*—geographical foci. The Book of Exodus is an example of different geographical foci. Israel is in Egypt (1–12), en route to Sinai (13–18), then gathered around Sinai (19–40). Additionally, the Book of Acts illustrates that a book may have parallel foci, both biographical and geographical (*cf.* Acts 1:8). Acts 1–7 transpires "in Jerusalem," 8:1–9:31 "throughout Judea, Galilee, and Samaria," 9:32–33 "as far as Phoenicia, Cyprus, and Antioch," 13:1–15:35 "throughout the region of Phrygia and Galatia," 15:36–21:16 "over to Macedonia," and 21:17–28:31 "to Rome."

   c. *Central events*—historical foci. The Book of Joshua is structured on Israel's two-pronged attack on Canaan: the first, the southern campaign in 1–10; the second, the northern campaign in 11–12; and the resultant allotment of land in 13–24.

---

33. Hermann Gunkel, *The Psalms* (Philadelphia: Fortress, 1967), 25.

HOW TO COMMUNICATE BIBLICAL CONTENT

d. *Central ideas*—ideological foci. The letter to Romans, the great doctrinal statement of New Testament Christianity, revolves around key ideas: 1–3, "for all have sinned," (or, *hamartiology*); 4–5, "being justified by faith," or soteriology; 6–8; "mortify the deeds of the flesh," or sanctification; 9–11 the predestination of Israel; and 12–16 guidelines for practical Christian living.

e. *Central times*—chronological foci. In some books, chronological features protrude, such as in 1 and 2 Kings, and 1 and 2 Chronicles. Of course, the key personages, the kings, also provide biographical foci.

2. *Look for Transitional Connectives and Dividers*. These serve to divide the book into major sections. Some structural dividers often provide inspired "tip-offs" for the book's sections.

a. *Repetition*—A repeated concept, sentence, or clause may serve to introduce or conclude a section. In the structure of Genesis, the sentence most repeated "the generations (or events) of" (2:4; 5:1; 10:1; 11:27), provides a heading or colophon for a new section. The nuclear phrase "and it came to pass that the word of the Lord came to Jonah" (1:2; 3:1) introduces the two sections of this narrative. 1 Corinthians is conveniently divided by the introductory phrase "now concerning," in 7:1, 25; 8:1; 12:1; and 16:1.[34] Each of the first five sections of the letter of James begins with "my brothers" or "my dear brothers": (1:2–18, 19–27; 2:1–13, 14–26; and 3:1–12). A repeated element, however, may also conclude a previous section. Similarly, the first three of the four major sections in Ecclesiastes conclude with "eat, drink, and find enjoyment in your work, for this is the gift of God" (2:24–26; 5:18–20; 8:15). The first five of the six major sections of Matthew conclude in a single

---

34. Kaiser, *Exegetical Theology*, 76.

temporal adverbial clause: "and it came to pass when Jesus had finished these sayings" (7:28; 11:1; 13:53; 19:1; 26:1).³⁵

b. *Terms*—Some conjunctions and connective adverbs may reveal a key transition between sections, such as: and, but, then, wherefore, therefore, nevertheless, before, meanwhile, afterward, and later. The key transitional "then" in Ephesians 4:1 introduces the change in content from doctrinal (1–3) to ethical (4–5); the transitional "finally" in 6:10 introduces the change in content from general ethics (4–5) to spiritual warfare (6:10ff.) In addition to signaling a transition, key terms may also characterize a particular section. Repeated terms within a section may provide a conceptual nucleus to distinguish the section from other sections in the book. For instance, the first four of the five major sections of Amos are characterized by different key terms. In the first section of Amos 1–2, the phrase "for three transgressions, even four" appears eight times. In Amos 3–5:17, the imperative "hear" signals the beginning of the section in 3:1 and is repeated in the course of the section in 5:1. The next section, 5:18–19, is characterized by the repeated "woe to you!" The fourth section of visions, Chapters 7–9, is marked by the repeated "the Lord God showed me" (7:1, 4, 7; 8:1; 9:1).³⁶ The final section of Amos on the restoration of Israel, 9:11–15, is marked by the introductory "in that day" (9:11), followed by the echo "the days are coming" (9:13).

c. *Questions*—A rhetorical question may signal a new section, or the repetition of a question(s) may structurally mark a section. The third section of Romans, Chapters 6–8, is introduced by the questions, "What shall we say then? Shall we sin that grace may abound?" The introductory questions are echoed by the abbreviated "What then?" in 6:15 and 7:7. The whole book of Malachi is actually a series of divine charges

---

35. Ibid., 73.
36. Ibid., 75.

to which Israel responds "in what" or "how have we sinned?" (1:2, 6, 7; 2:14, 17; 3:8, 13).[37]

d. *Vocative*—In some cases (often in epistolary literature), a new section begins through a change in a form of address that shifts attention from one group to another to begin a new section. The three sections of Micah, beginning in 1:2; 3:1 and 6:1, respectively, each begin with "hear," but "hear" is addressed first to "all peoples of the earth," then to "heads of Jacob, the rulers of the house of Israel," and finally to the mountains to act as judge and jury against the criminal defendant, Israel.[38] Three sections in James, 4:1–12, 4:13–17, and 5:1–6, are marked by vocative changes, "you adulterous people" (4:4), "now listen, you who say" (4:13), and "now listen, you rich people" (5:1).

e. *Change in time, mood, and/or setting*—Ezra 1–6 and 7–10 are divided by a time change that takes place between the reign of King Darius (*cf.* 6:13) and the reign of King Artaxerxes (7:1, "now after these things, during the reign of Artaxerxes"). A dramatic change in mood and atmosphere is illustrated in Psalm 1: In Psalm 1:1–3 the mood is tranquil, bucolic and serene; verses 4–6 are dark, heavy and foreboding. A change of setting is a favorite device of narrative writers, and this also may indicate a new section. In 1 Kings 17:1–7, Elijah is before Ahab and then in his retreat by the brook Cherith. In 17:8–24, he is with the widow at Zarephath. Later, Elijah joins Obadiah in Samaria in 18:1–15, and ascends Mount Carmel to his confrontation with false prophets of Baal in 18:16–46. Finally, Elijah, in his divine encounter, is restored and comforted at Horeb in 19:1–18. Each of these five sections is distinguished by a different setting.

f. *Content alone*—The ultimate informant of what constitutes a distinct section is its content, and in some cases, a change in content is the only "tip-off" of a different section. For instance,

---

37. Ibid., 74.
38. Ibid.

Revelation 2–3 is clearly outlined by the various Churches to whom Christ prophesies. Revelation 4–5 is John's vision of the Lamb of God. This example contains sharp differences in content as well as style to indicate the different sections.

The following is an example of a structural relation between sections of a book:
An introverted or chiastic structure in 1 Corinthians 11–14:

A—11:2-16 Women in submission

   B—11:17-34 Come to together to eat

      C—12:1-11 Gifts in general

         D—12:12-30 Diversity in unity

         D`—13:1-13 Charity in unity

      C`—14:1-25 Gifts in particular: tongues/prophecy

   B`—14:26-33a Come together to worship

A`—14:33b-40 Women in submission

One particular study tool, E. W. Bullinger's *The Companion Bible*, is extremely helpful for the exegete in that it provides structural treatment of every book of the Bible, every section of every book of the Bible, and almost every paragraph of the Bible. Every passage is outlined similarly to the one above to illustrate the internal structural relations that are referred to as "deep structure," and Bullinger's deep structural analysis will provide a plethora of observations for the exegete.

The observation of structural focal points and structural connectives and dividers should provide fuel (i.e., subjects and complements) for preaching points. For instance, in Ephesians 1–3, God's work for the saved is disclosed; in Ephesians 4–6, the saved in their obedience to God is disclosed. The former may constitute a subject and the latter a complement: "Since God works for you, therefore work for him." Similarly, Hebrews 1–10 describes how the Old Testament faith has been completed in Christ; 11–13 enjoins faithfulness to the finished faith. A preaching point here might be "be faithful to the finished faith."[39] God designed the books He authored to be coherent, and their coherence to be effected by some unifying thesis. The thesis of an entire book, in turn used as a thesis for a sermon, allows the hearers the opportunity for a bird's eye view of God's design. A basic logic underlies the surface structure of any book of the Bible; discovering of that logic, then summarizing it into a single, relevant sentence that is applicable to the people, and finally developing it with supporting material derived from the book is an unusual—but extremely profitable—task for a sermon.

2.1C Observe the entire book, particularly the relations between paragraphs in sequence and interrelations between paragraphs out of sequence

The Relation Between Paragraphs

The following is a list of typical logical or literary relations between paragraphs. Because the relations between paragraphs are conceptual, perhaps involving numerous intricacies and nuances, the categories should not be viewed as Procrustes' beds. The relation between paragraphs may involve more than one category.

The relations between paragraphs are important because they are the "joints" of the skeleton of a book of the Bible. If the exegete can think through the book paragraph by paragraph, allowing his mind to "snake" through all the transitions between paragraphs, he is then ready to begin the observational process in detail—viewing paragraphs as a whole, sentence sequences, and words in sentences.

The following list of paragraph relations should be observed in two ways: (1) as relations between adjacent paragraphs—that is, the relation between the paragraph and the preceding paragraph (if any), as well as the relation between the paragraph and the

---

39. Rev. Dr. Mark Minnick unpublished sermon, Survey of the Book of Hebrews, Mount Calvary Baptist Church, Greenville, S.C., Fall, '80.

following one (in any); and (2) with other paragraphs in the book that are not necessarily in sequence. These laws should be applied in order, first between paragraphs in sequence, and then between paragraphs out of sequence, since examining paragraph interrelations within divisions of a book, or throughout the book as a whole, gives the preacher a "feel" for the context that is essential to a balanced handling of any text.[40]

Relations of Continuity and Similarity

[1] *Repetition*—The same terms, phrases, clauses, concepts, or doctrines are repeated—in Leviticus, numerous paragraphs are tied together by like terms or ideas: "sacrifice," "holy," "I am the Lord."[41]

[2] *Continuation*—The same basic "core" concept is continued, but new perspectives are added to the same central doctrine—the parables of Matthew 13 all concern the "nature of the true spiritual kingdom," but each adds a new perspective to their common subject.[42]

[3] *Harmony/interchange*—Often paragraphs out of sequence repeat similar elements—sin in Romans 1:18–31 and Romans 3:21ff.[43]

[4] *Completion*—The paragraph brings to a resolution what has preceded. Joseph revealing himself to his brothers; Lot's sin with his daughters.[44]

[5] *Climax*—In some cases, paragraphs are arranged so that the last of them constitutes the ultimate in its section's development—Exodus 40:34–35 and Revelation 22.[45]

---

40. Compare Robert A. Traina, *Methodical Bible Study* (New York: Ganis and Horns, 1952), 49ff.
41. Ibid.
42. Ibid.
43. Ibid.
44. Ibid.
45. Ibid.

HOW TO COMMUNICATE BIBLICAL CONTENT

Relations of Discontinuity and Dissimilarity

[1] *Comparison*—Two or more paragraphs serve to compare different aspects of a subject—Hebrews 5:1-4 and 5:5-10 illustrate a clear comparative relationship between paragraphs.[46]

[2] *Contrast*—Two or more paragraphs contrast opposite factors. Cain and Abel in Genesis 4; Eli and his sons in 1 Samuel 3.

[3] *Cruciality*—The contour of the text pivots at this point. This is a major crux or turning point. After 2 Samuel 11, the whole narrative revolves around David's sin and its consequences.[47]

Relations of Logical Development

[1] *Particularization*—Matthew 5:13-16 deals with general terms such as salt and light, while the previous and subsequent paragraphs deal with specific aspects of life in the kingdom.[48]

[2] *Generalization*—The same illustration above demonstrates the development from the specific in Matthew 5:1-11 to the general in 13-16.[49]

[3] *Explanation*—In Matthew 13, the parable of the sower (or rather, the soils) is later interpreted by Christ; in Mark 4, there is a similar example of parable followed by explanation.[50]

[4] *Interrogation*—a question and answer structure. "Adam where art thou?" in Genesis 3; rhetorical questions in Romans Chapters 6-8.[51]

[5] *Point/counterpoint*—a debate style format where a point is made, then an objection is anticipated and rebutted. In 1

46. Ibid.
47. Ibid.
48. Ibid.
49. Ibid.
50. Ibid.
51. Ibid.

Corinthians 15, Paul declares the resurrection; then quotes an objection, "How can the dead rise?"; then refutes the objection.[52]

[6] *Cause/effect*—In Romans 1:18ff., Paul outlines the reason (or cause) for man's ignorance of God (the effect).[53]

[7] *Summarization*—a compendium or abridgment of previous material. Joshua 12 includes a summary of the military campaign against Canaan.[54]

In a relation of two paragraphs in sequence and/or an interrelation of two paragraphs out of sequence, it is conceivable that any one paragraph may provide a subject and another its complement. For instance, Romans 3:19–20 may provide the subject—the impossibility of the law saving anyone. Romans 3:21–25 may provide the complement—the atonement of Christ effecting salvation. A valid preaching point may be "it is Christ's atoning, not your law-keeping, that saves you." Another example may be taken from Psalm 95. The first of the two paragraphs in this Psalm may provide a subject—the blessedness of worshipping God; the latter of the two paragraphs may provide a complement—the danger of a hardened heart. A valid preaching point from these two paragraphs (which in this case would constitute the scope of the whole Psalm) may be "the blessedness of worship may be destroyed by hardness of heart."

2.1D DETERMINE THE BOOK'S SUBJECT THROUGH OBSERVING WHAT ALL THE SECTIONS AND PARAGRAPHS HAVE IN COMMON, AND THE BOOK'S COMPLEMENT BY OBSERVING WHAT IS DISTINCT TO EACH OF THE SECTIONS

The Book's Subject

52. Ibid.
53. Ibid.
54. Ibid.

If the exegete can think through the entire book paragraph by paragraph, including the relations of the paragraphs in sequence, the discovery of the book's subject is readily accessible. The book's subject is simply that concept, expressed in a single phrase, that is covered by all the book's sections and paragraphs; the book's all-encompassing subject is whichever thread runs through each section and paragraph and is the binding cord of the entire book.

The Book's Complement

Each main section of the book provides a complementary idea that completes the central subject. Therefore, to the central book subject there are many complements, corresponding to each section. The fusion of these complements together is the book complement. For instance, in Romans, the concept of the righteousness of God permeates each section and paragraph—this is the book subject. Romans 1–3 has the complement, "the universality of sin"; Romans 4–5, "how righteousness is imputed by faith"; Romans 6–8, "how righteousness is imparted in sanctification"; Romans 9–11, "how righteousness is dispensed by the sovereign will of God"; and Romans 12–16, "how righteousness is lived out in practical life." Fusing these five complements together may result in the phrase "salvation and sanctification." Thus, the book's subject/complement may be "God's righteousness saves and sanctifies believers" or "the righteousness of God is the basis of salvation." As each section of a book provides a complement to the book's subject, so each paragraph provides a complement to the unifying idea of the section. In other words, the subject/complement relationship applies. When proceeding to further analyze and outline a book, the complements in each book-section are themselves subjects which are completed by the ideas in the paragraphs. Thus, the section/paragraph relationship is similarly a subject/complement relationship. These subject/complement relationships may provide the substance for preaching points.[55]

---

55. For exercises that would allow the exegete to practice the skill of determining subjects and complements, see Haddon Robinson, *Expository Preaching*. Although the exercises are on the passage level rather than the book level,

For instance, a preaching point covering the whole content of the book of Romans might be "the righteousness of the God is your salvation." Communication of this point, for instance, could involve use of the five developmental questions:

(1) What does this mean?

(2) Is it true?

(3) What does it look like?

(4) How may we be encouraged to believe and obey it?

(5) How does it change me in real life?

The exegete/homilist may first explain righteousness and salvation by defining each term:

(1) Since, in Romans, salvation includes sanctification, an explanation of salvation with its parts in Romans—substitution (3:21ff), justification (4–5), sanctification (6–8), and predestination (9–11)—would be appropriate.

(2) Then the exegete/homilist could argue the validity of the point—arguing that all men need righteousness, for all have sinned (1–3).

(3) The matter of giving righteousness could be illustrated through the image of a judge acquitting the guilty.

(4) The homilist may then encourage those who do not have God's gift of righteousness to seek it.

(5) The homilist may briefly describe how the imputed righteousness of God will change one's life.

---

the skills acquired through working with passages readily apply to working with whole books. Further, the Dallas Theological Seminary library includes numerous book syntheses by Th.D. students which include book subject and complement discussions.

2.1E Consult key synthetic tools and revise the book's subject/complement, if necessary

Key Synthetic Tools

"Synthesis" literally means "to put together;" "analysis" literally means "to take apart." When the exegete struggles with the content of a book of the Bible, the exegete must synthesize the content of the book into a single subject/complement. The following is a list of the key synthetic tools. These works are not commentaries, per se; they are works that summarize and synthesize the contents of each book of the Bible:

Baxter, Sidlow. *The Strategic Grasp of the Bible.*

Brooks, Philip. *The Summarized Bible.*

Geisler, Norman. *Christ in the Bible.*

Gundry, Robert William. *A Survey of the Bible.*

Jensen, Irving L. *Survey of the OT.*

Jensen, Irving L. *Survey of the NT.*

Morgan, G. Campbell. *The Analyzed Bible.*

Morgan, G. Campbell. *The Message of the Bible.*

Scroggie, Graham. *Know Your Bible.*

Scroggie, Graham. *The Unfolding Drama of Redemption.*

Sleming, D. *Survey of the Bible.*

Wilkinson and Boa. *Walk through the Bible.*

The synthetic tools listed above are valuable for several reasons:

(1) They confirm whether or not the exegete's perception of the book overall thesis is "on target" or "in the ball park."

(2) They allow the exegete to sharpen and improve his phraseology, to obtain a thesis that is not only the most accurate but also the best sounding.

EXPOUNDING THE GOSPEL AND LAW OF GOD

(3) They may bring to the exegete's attention matters for observation of which he has previously been unaware.

Further, the better exegetical commentaries include introductions, which may provide a profound a "bird's eye" view, with brevity. The perspective at this phase of exegesis is macroscopic overview, not microscopic scrutiny, and for this particular exegetical purpose, the exegete need not become bogged down with lengthy or detailed discussion. Those works which communicate the most through the fewest words are the most valuable to provide a bird's eye synopsis. Once exegetes can see the forests, they can then proceed to dissect individual trees.

2.1F Record the fruits of the book overview with an analytical chart

An analytical chart is a "snap shot" of the entire book of the Bible, providing the exegete with a "bird's eye" view. The chart may be as general or as specific as the exegete needs. Genesis, may be charted in the following simple display:

Universal/Global 1–11	National/Ethnic 12–50
Cosmic Focus 1	Abraham 12–25
Creation 1–2	Isaac 26–27
Fall 3	Jacob 28–35
Murder 4	Esau 36
Geneology 5	Antrhropological Focus 2
Flood 6–9	Joseph 37–50
Languages And Nations 10–11	

2.2 Observe the Entire Paragraph in the Original Language

Why Study the Bible Paragraph by Paragraph?

The paragraph, rather than the word, phrase, clause, or sentence, is the basic unit of Bible study. Words appear in phrases, phrases in clauses, and clauses in sentences. Even a sentence, however, requires a context to determine its meaning accurately, and observing sentences out of sequence risks incorrect interpretation. Therefore, a paragraph is the native environment for sentences; the paragraph provides an element of contextual completion that the lesser segments of Scripture do not supply.

Why Study Paragraphs in the Original Language?

The original text of Scripture, that which God directly breathed out (2 Tim. 3:16-17), is, to use an analogy, three-dimensional; if the original were placed before a mirror, the mirror should accurately reflect the contour and nature of the original. However, it would still be a two-dimensional image. To use a similar analogy, some television programming has been specially designed for three-dimensional viewing with special glasses. A knowledge of the original languages is the tool that provides such an in-depth viewing of the Scriptures; without such a tool, the Bible can be observed accurately—but within limits. There is simply no substitute for observing what God wrote, the way God wrote it. This does not mean that those who rely on translations are doomed to theological mediocrity. To the contrary, the ranks of those who theologized solely from translations and commentaries include John Bunyan and D. Martin Lloyd-Jones. Even so, knowledge of the original language is a tool to facilitate more accurate study and more efficient use of time in interpretation.

Hebrew, Aramaic and Greek Are the Languages of Divine Choice

The fact that God chose specific languages through which to communicate implies an element of divine regard for those languages. The versatility of Semitic literary forms—narrative, poetry, psalm, and prophecy—suit the manifold designs of God the Communicator. The brief Aramaic segments of the Old Testament—Gen. 31:47; Jer. 10:11; Ezra 7:12–26; and Daniel 2:4b–7:28—are Semitic as well; the use of Aramaic in the section of Daniel on the nations implies that God was beginning the transition to communicate to all nations equally. Greek, due to the philosophical and intellectual development of Greek luminaries, entered a new dimension of linguistic definition: this language was particularly suited as a vehicle to communicate philosophical concepts. The extremely accurate nature of the Greek language, and the near universality of its use in the first century, imply that theological concepts were to be defined with a new and higher accuracy in the New Testament, and that God's revelation was now to be directed to all nations (*cf.* Eph. 2:1–11).

2.2A ANALYZE THE PARAGRAPH

(1) Form a mechanical layout that delineates phrases, clauses, sentences, and logical relations between sentences.

The Mechanical Layout: The Schematic Display of Propositions

What is a mechanical layout? A mechanical layout is simply the rewriting of the text with the purpose of visualizing the thought flow of the author more readily. To grasp a paragraph, the exegete must be able to think the author's thoughts after him. The mechanical layout (also referred to as the *propositional display* or clausal structural layout, as it is called in Beekman and Callow's *Translating the Word of God*) can help trace the author's thoughts.[56] For the pur-

---

56. For various "mechanical layouts" or "schematic displays," see Walter Kaiser, *Towards an Exegetical Theology* (Grand Rapids: Baker, 1981), 165–81;

poses of this thesis, a mechanical layout will refer to a schematic display of the sentences and clauses in a passage, and "structural layout" will refer to a schematic display of the conceptual structure of a passage (to be discussed *infra* in part (2) of this section). A schematic display of clauses aids the exegete to trace the author's line of reasoning and ascertain his flow of argument.

How to Set Up a Mechanical Layout

The following is a step-by-step procedure to set up the mechanical layout. After following this procedure a few times, the exegete may be able to construct such layouts as a matter of second nature.

[1] Each sentence, whether indicative, subjunctive, imperative, optative or interrogatory, should be placed on the extreme left-hand margin of the page; this includes all independent clauses, even if they are coordinate (i.e., those clauses connected by conjunctions).

[2] Each line on the far left-hand margin includes all its modifiers, unless there is more than one modifier (in which case they are listed vertically) or unless a modifier is unusually long (in which case it will be divided).

[3] Each subordinate clause is placed to the right of the independent clause it modifies.

[4] Two or more modifiers, whether they are subordinate clauses, phrases or words, should be placed on the right of the left margin in vertical configuration.

[5] Any list, whether of persons, places, things, things, qualities, or adjectives, should be listed in vertical columns for clarity.[57]

Walter Kaiser, *Malachi: God's Unchanging Love* (Grand Rapids: Baker, 1984), 188ff.

57. This guide for a mechanical layout is an adaption of unpublished class notes from Howard Hendricks, Dallas Theological Seminary, "301—Hermeneutics and Bible Study," Fall, 1987.

EXPOUNDING THE GOSPEL AND LAW OF GOD

An excellent introduction to the art of establishing a mechanical layout is in Merrill C. Tenney's commentary on Galatians, in the chapter "Analyzing the Text."[58]

The Mechanical Layout: The Logical Relations between Propositions

What are logical relations between propositions? As outlined in 2.2c, paragraphs have discernible relations between those in sequence and interrelations between those not in sequence. Similarly, propositions within paragraphs have logical relations. After the propositions have been schematically displayed, it should be more easily discerned how the propositions relate to each other. The "six faithful men"—what, where, when, why and how—are helpful points to initiate consideration of how propositions relate. These initial questions may be asked to determine how the propositions fit together. However, the exegete may simply define and label how these propositions fit according to his own perception.

A Mechanical Layout Illustrated from Philippians 1:9-11

The following text of Philippians 1:9-11 (ESV) provides the exegete with a "thought flow" of the author's argument. By copying and pasting the text, and simply utilizing the tab feature, the exegete may mechanically lay out, visually, the thought flow of the passage.

Phil. 1:9 And

it is my prayer	SUBJECT
that your love may abound more and more,	EXPANSION
with knowledge and	CONTENT
all discernment, [10]	CONTENT
so that you may approve what is excellent,	RESULT
and so be pure and blameless	SPECIFIC
for the day of Christ,	TELOS
[11] filled with the fruit of righteousness	RESULT

---

58. Merrill C. Tenney, *Galatians: The Charter of Christian Liberty* (Grand Rapids: Eerdmans), 165-85.

> that comes through Jesus Christ,   MEANS
> to the glory and praise of God.   TELOS

(2) Form a structural layout that identifies deep structure.

Whereas the mechanical layout is linear and forward-looking in focus, the structural layout focuses on the internal, deep structure of the passage. The following structural diagram illustrates a possible view of the deep structure of Philippians 1:9–11.

> A—Phil. 1:9 And it is my prayer
>> B—that your love may abound more and more,
>>> C—with knowledge and all discernment,
>>>> D—10 so that you may approve what is excellent,
>>> C`—and so be pure and blameless for the day of Christ,
>> B`—11 filled with the fruit of righteousness that comes through Jesus Christ,
> A`—to the glory and praise of God.

This structural inversion hinges on "D" where Paul turns on the crucial focus that believers be able to approve, that is discern and apprehend, whatever is good and excellent. When a believer prays, as per "A", they pray, ultimately, to the praise and glory of God, as per "A`". Pursuant to "B" and "B`", the believers' love increases more and more, so that they are filled with the fruit of righteousness. (Love is the first fruit of the Spirit listed in Galatians 5:22.) The means of apprehension of what is good and excellent is according to "C", with the result of such apprehension being purity and blamelessness on and unto the day of Christ, as per "C`."

(3) Form a grammatical diagram.

Once the exegete has ordered the passage into a mechanical layout for a linear, forward-looking focus, and the passage into a structural layout, for its internal, deep structure, the exegete may proceed to linguistic, grammatical diagram.

EXPOUNDING THE GOSPEL AND LAW OF GOD

The Greek text of Philippians 1:9-11 reads as follows:

9 Καὶ τοῦτο προσεύχομαι, ἵνα ἡ ἀγάπη ὑμῶν ἔτι μᾶλλον καὶ μᾶλλον περισσεύῃ ἐν ἐπιγνώσει καὶ πάσῃ αἰσθήσει 10 εἰς τὸ δοκιμάζειν ὑμᾶς τὰ διαφέροντα, ἵνα ἦτε εἰλικρινεῖς καὶ ἀπρόσκοποι εἰς ἡμέραν Χριστοῦ, 11 πεπληρωμένοι καρπὸν δικαιοσύνης τὸν διὰ Ἰησοῦ Χριστοῦ εἰς δόξαν καὶ ἔπαινον θεοῦ.

This text may be diagrammed as follows:

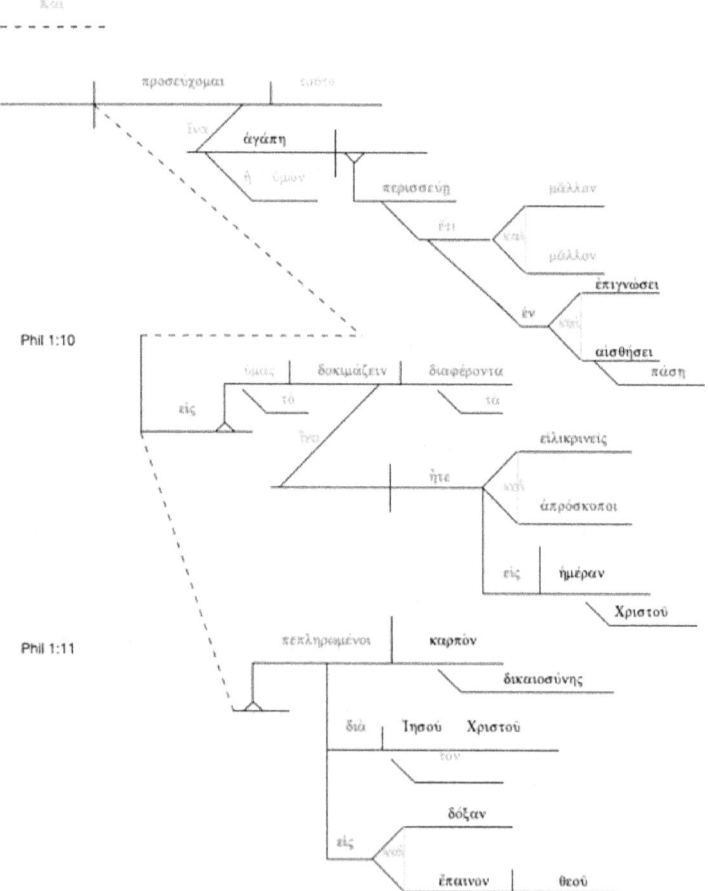

2.2B INTERPRET FINDINGS

(1) Interpret all syntactical relationships.

Once the exegete has completed the linguistic, grammatical diagram, the exegete has a visual work station to analyze syntax. What is syntax? While grammar is the actual linguistic form of a particular word in the text, syntax is the actual sense of that particular word in the immediate context. For instance, in Colossians 3:16 Paul exhorts, "let the Word of Christ dwell in you richly, singing to yourselves in psalms, hymns, and spiritual songs ..." "Of Christ" is a genitive grammatically. Syntactically, the genitive could be a subjective genitive or an objective genitive. A subjective genitive would be interpreted as Christ, as a subject, speaking. To be sure, in the context of singing the Psalms, Christ would be speaking through the Psalms. However, since Psalms also refer to Christ, an objective genitive would convey the sense that the object of the Word is Christ. Certainly, both syntactical categories may be true. The exegete needs syntactical senses of at least every key word in the text, if not all the words.

The Standard Syntactical Works

The matter of syntactical categories has been addressed in a variety of grammatical works.

Hebrew:

Arnold, Bill T., and John H. Choi. *A Guide to Biblical Hebrew Syntax*. Cambridge: Cambridge University Press, 2003. Defines the fundamental syntactical features of the Hebrew Bible and provides examples with English translations. This work is not a complete reference grammar; instead, its logical organization and simple explanations make it an ideal quick reference and invaluable help in understanding key concepts.

Chisholm, Jr., Robert B. *A Workbook for Intermediate Hebrew: Grammar, Exegesis, and Commentary on Jonah and Ruth*. Grand Rapids, MI: Kregel Publications, 2006. A workbook for use in conjunction with standard Hebrew grammar references, offering

87

practical exercises to reinforce patterns and principles of Hebrew grammar and syntax. Includes references to Pratico and Van Pelt within the text and numerous additional references in the footnotes. Parsing guide and glossary are also included.

Gibson, J. C. L., ed. *Davidson's Introductory Hebrew Grammar—Syntax*. 4th ed. Edinburgh: T. and T. Clark, 1994. The greatly expanded fourth edition of a timeless classic, written to benefit advanced students and teachers of biblical Hebrew. Includes an extensive bibliography and several useful indexes from which the reader may draw resources for further study.

Jouon, Paul, and T. Muraoka. *A Grammar of Biblical Hebrew (Subsidia Biblica)*. 2nd ed. Rome: Biblical Institute Press, 2006. This reference grammar does not contain the exhaustive detail of *Gesenius*, but its contemporary treatments and form offer the reader greater accessibility and more accurate textual interpretations.

Kautzsch, E., ed. *Gesenius' Hebrew Grammar*. 2nd ed. Translated by A. E. Cowley. New York: Oxford University Press, 1910. This classic reference grammar has largely been replaced by Jouon and Muraoka.

Putnam, Frederic Clarke, ed. *A Cumulative Index to the Grammar and Syntax of Biblical Hebrew*. Winona Lake, IN: Eisenbrauns, 1996. A comprehensive index, organized by scripture verse, of examples found in major grammars and syntaxes. Especially useful in locating discussions of problematic passages.

van der Merwe, Christo H. J., Jackie A. Naude, and Jan H. Kroeze. *A Biblical Hebrew Reference Grammar*. Sheffield, England: Sheffield Academic Press, 1999. By incorporating recent advances in Biblical Hebrew syntactical structures, this work enables translation of textual units beyond those presented by traditional sentence-grammar studies.

Waltke, Bruce K., and M. O'Connor. *An Introduction to Biblical Hebrew Syntax*. Winona Lake, IN: Eisenbrauns, 1990. This work provides a much-needed update to *Gesenius*. Organized as a reference, but equally useful for use in self-guided study, its comprehensive coverage of sentence interpretation and thorough inclusion of secondary literature make Waltke and O'Connor standard reading for exegetes who desire to move beyond basic Hebrew for a greater understanding of the text. Provides over 3,500 Biblical Hebrew examples, an abundance of footnotes, and an amazing table of authorities from which the reader may draw resources for further specialized study.

Williams, Ronald J. *Williams' Hebrew Syntax*, 3rd ed. Edited by John C. Beckman. Toronto: University of Toronto Press Inc., 2007. A revised and expanded version of Ronald J. Williams' *Hebrew Syntax: An Outline*. Provides explanations of grammatical categories, cross-referenced with corresponding sections of the major reference grammars. Interlinear English translations are included for all Hebrew phrases and sentences, and all examples are interpreted using both literal and idiomatic translations. A classic work that has largely been replaced by Waltke and O'Connor.

Greek:

Brooks, James A., and Carlton L. Winbery. *The Syntax of New Testament Greek*. Lanham, MD: University Press of America, 1978. A well-presented and practical introduction to New Testament Greek syntax. Offers concise explanations and an abundance of examples. Best used to supplement traditional grammars to gain a more thorough understanding of the main grammatical categories.

Dana, Harvey Eugene, and Julius R. Mantey. *A Manual of Grammar of the Greek New Testament*. New York: McMillian Company, 1927. Usually referred to as "Dana and Mantey," this classic work provides a basis for understanding Biblical Greek grammar. Daniel Wallace's *Greek Grammar Beyond the Basics: An Exegetical Syntax of the New Testament* (below) provides a more modern alternative.

Robertson, A. T. *A Grammar of the Greek New Testament in the Light of Historical Research*, 4th ed. Nashville: Broadman Press, 1934. An important and beautifully written book, containing 1,500 pages of noteworthy scholarship. Despite being slightly dated due to advances in syntactic interpretation, this work remains among the best resources available to advanced students and teachers of New Testament Greek who desire to attain mastery. Provides many examples, all without English translations.

Wallace, Daniel B. *The Basics of New Testament Syntax: An Intermediate Greek Grammar*. Grand Rapids, MI: Zondervan, 2009. While Wallace's larger *Greek Grammar Beyond the Basics: An Exegetical Syntax of the New Testament* is the preferred reference, this abridgement offers guidance that is both precise and portable. Thoroughly cross-referenced to *Exegetical Syntax*, this book includes discussions and answer keys related to all semantic categories, and numerous charts and tables for greater reader accessibility.

Wallace, Daniel B. *Greek Grammar Beyond the Basics: An Exegetical Syntax of the New Testament*. Grand Rapids, MI: Zondervan, 1997. Ground-breaking textbook by Dallas Theological Seminary professor and noted textual critic, Daniel B. Wallace. Explores numerous syntactical categories for the simplification and classification of Greek grammatical usages, systematically linking syntax and exegesis for more accurate and sound textual interpretations. Contains a subject index, a Greek word index, and page numbers in the Syntax Summary section, none of which are available in the abridgement.

Wallace, Daniel B., and Grant G. Edwards. *A Workbook for New Testament Syntax: Companion to Basics of New Testament Syntax and Greek Grammar Beyond the Basics: An Exegetical Syntax of the New Testament*. Grand Rapids, MI: Zondervan, 2007. Workbook to accompany Wallace's books. Exposes students to the use of syntactical categories in the interpretation of significant passages.

The standard abridged works, which allow for ease of usage, are, for the Hebrew, Williams' *Hebrew Syntax: An Outline* and Davidson's *Hebrew Grammar*, and for the Greek, Dana and Mantey's *A Manual Grammar of the Greek New Testament*. Waltke's Hebrew grammar is too complex for most exegetes; the average exegete, however, can use Waltke's work as a textual commentary by using its index to find treatments of texts under consideration. If the exegete uses the standard syntactical works regularly, the categories should become second nature, even memorized. For the Greek, the brilliant New Testament scholar Dan Wallace's works on Greek syntax are standards in the field. Jouon's, Davidson's, and Waltke's works remain standards in the Old Testament field.

To adequately discern the nuances of the paragraph under consideration, the exegete should determine the syntactical category of each word of each sentence in the paragraph. Because the nuance of each word in a sentence affects the overall meaning of a sentence, the time required for the exegete to "pin down" the precise nuance of each word is worthwhile. Because the matters of syntax are adequately treated in the Hebrew by Davidson and in Greek by Dana and Mantey, this work will not offer a full treatment of syntactical categories. To later illustrate, however, a method for exegetical outlining, this work will offer the following treatment of the syntax of Hebrew and Greek structural markers. Structural markers are the most significant terms or constructions that structure a Scripture author's flow of argument. Structural markers provide the "nerve centers" of the paragraph. The most important structural markers are main verbs. Three other constructions are always important structural markers: circumstantial (adverbial) participles, adverbial infinitives, and subordinate conjunctions.

Some prepositional phrases may be strategic enough in a paragraph to serve as structural markers. In the case of prepositional phrases, the exegete will have to determine which prepositional phrases constitute a "nerve center" of a paragraph. Main verbs, adverbial participles, adverbial infinitives, and subordinate conjunctions are always important structural markers in both Hebrew (as well as Aramaic) and Greek.

(2) Interpret figures of speech using the grammatical diagram.
Words have different levels of meaning, the encyclopedic, grammatical, syntactical, literal, and figurative. (1) The encyclopedic level covers the word in all of its nuances, as a lexicon would list the various meanings if there are more than one. This is the beginning

level of meaning to consider when exegeting because it offers the various options of what the word may mean in a particular context. (2) The grammatical level shows what grammatical form the word takes. For instance, the verb "show" may take the grammatical form "I show," "he shows," "they showed," or "it will show." At this level, the exegete must correctly grammatically analyze each word. This grammatical analysis is commonly called parsing or locating. (3) The syntactical level of meaning is the specific nuance of the word connoted by the context. For instance, when Jesus stated, "The Son of Man is delivered into the hands of sinners," he used the verb "is delivered" in the present grammatical tense. The action of the verb, however, had not yet occurred. Therefore, he used the verb as grammatically present but syntactically future. Although the form of the verb would show it to be present, the context would show it to be future.

(4) The literal and (5) figurative senses of words interrelate. For instance, in Hebrew the term usually referring to the innermost being is literally "kidneys." In this case the typical meaning of the term is on the figurative level rather than the literal. Figures of speech produce word images or word pictures. One particular scholar, Meir Weiss, after treatments of words in context and phrases, offers a lengthy treatment of images, or word pictures. Although some linguists see images as didactic devices that clarify the subject matter, others, such as Aristotle, saw images as the core of poetic language. One Rabbinic commentator, Rabbi Judah, attacked literalistic denial of word images—"whoever translates a verse literally is a liar." Rabbi Judah argued that word images are integral parts of interpretation. Similarly, in the sixteenth, seventeenth, and eighteenth centuries they were viewed "like cherries tastefully arranged on a cake." Actually, a word image may be a "grace or ornament or added power of language." Metaphors or word images in a particular context must be understood in order to trace the author's flow of argument.

The New Testament department at Dallas Theological Seminary defines a word image or figure of speech in more specific terms:

HOW TO COMMUNICATE BIBLICAL CONTENT

A figure of speech is a word, phrase, or sentence that is cast in an unusual form to denote a meaning that is different from its customary usage but is considered appropriate by analogy. That is, a word or phrase is used out of its ordinary sense, place, or manner for the purpose of attracting our attention to what is being said. The demands of context help us determine whether the words are being used literally or figuratively. The truth conveyed by the words is literal though the words employed may be figurative.[59]

The following is a sampling of various figures of speech. The list may give the exegete a taste for figure of speech categories. However, the "be all and end all" of figure of speech categories is Bullinger's *Figures of Speech*. The exegete should utilize the index of this work regularly on whatever text considered. Considering figures of speech, and understanding their conceptual import, is a "must." Bullinger's *Figures of Speech* may be used profitably in either of two ways—first, as a textual commentary and second, as a reference source for categories of figures. As a textual commentary, simply use the index in the back of *Figures of Speech* to determine if Bullinger actually treated the figures in the verse under consideration. Using the index of Bullinger's *Figures of Speech* in the Bible may be the best way for the beginning exegete to become familiar with the various figure of speech categories.

After the beginner exegete has acquired the skill of identifying the categories, the exegete may consider tabbing Bullinger's *Figures of Speech* in order to refer to similar categories. The exegete may find recurring trends in the use of a particular figure of speech. For instance, private areas of the body are often referred to euphemistically through figures of speech. Leviticus, for instance, orders Israelites to "wash their flesh with water" (Lev. 14–15). This recurring euphemism may lead the exegete to conclude that God does not condone graphic depiction of personal and private parts of the human anatomy.

---

59. Unpublished class notes, "204—Exegetical Method in Ephesians," Dallas Theological Seminary, Spring, 1988.

A Sampling of Major Figures of Speech
Figures of Speech That Compare Ideas
Simile

A simile is a figure of speech that compares two entities, usually through the propositions "like" or "as." The purpose of the comparison is to clarify or explain a particular truth. Usually one of the compared entities is a well-known quantity. The less clear entity is explained or clarified by the more common entity. Some parables which use the prepositions "like" or "as" in order to bridge the comparison have been called extended similes.[60]

Examples of similes include Matthew 9:36 and Matthew 28:4, respectively. "The guards shook with fear and became like dead men." And, "they were scattered as sheep having no shepherd."[61]

Metaphor

A metaphor is a comparison of two essentially dissimilar entities. One entity is explained or clarified by some point of correspondence with another entity. The likeness or analogy between the two entities explains or clarifies. It is a figure that makes a truth clearer by stating that one thing represents or is defined by another object because of a likeness or analogy between the two. Allegory and type are extended metaphors.[62]

Examples of metaphor include, respectively, Matthew 15:13 and 16:6. "Every plant which my Father did not plant shall be rooted up." Here Jesus compared religious authority figures and religious power structures to "plants." "Beware of the leaven of the Pharisees."[63] Jesus compared the doctrinal and ethical teachings of the Pharisees to leaven. As leavens spreads, so do false theology and ethics.

Figures of Speech That Substitute One Idea for Another Idea

60. Ibid.
61. Ibid.
62. Ibid.
63. Ibid.

HOW TO COMMUNICATE BIBLICAL CONTENT

Metonymy

When two entities are commonly associated together, an author may sometimes refer to one entity by naming the other entity. Because of frequent association between the two entities, the name of one entity is used to suggest another. The entities commonly associated together usually have one of the four logical relationships: (1) cause substitutes for effect, (2) effect substitutes for cause, (3) an accouterment related to a subject substitutes for that subject, (4) an adjunct related to a subject substitutes for the subject.[64]

Examples of the four metonymical relationships are as follows: In Acts 7:8, an adjunct related to a subject substitutes for Stephen's subject: "He gave him the covenant of circumcision." Circumcision was an outward sign of the Abrahamic covenant. Here Stephen substituted a key component or adjunct of the Abrahamic covenant as a whole. In Deuteronomy 28:5, accouterments readily associated with daily life in Moses' era represent the whole of daily life. "Blessed shall be your basket and your kneading bowl." In Acts 1:18, Luke narrates that Judas "burst open in the middle." The result of his falling was his injury. The cause of the injury was Judas' falling. Here, the result substitutes for the cause. In Luke 16:29, Jesus describes the Scriptures as "Moses and the Prophets"—"They have Moses and the Prophets, let them hear them."[65] The authors or human causes of the Scriptures substitute for the Scriptures themselves.

Synecdoche

A synecdoche is a communication of the whole by only naming the part. This is the usual form of synecdoche. Also, a synecdoche may occur when the part is communicated while naming the whole. Judas confessed that "I have sinned by betraying innocent blood" in Matthew 27:4. Judas communicated that he betrayed the Lord by naming only the part. His choice of synecdoche underscores that wrongful death inflicted on Christ. Paul used synecdoche in 1

---

64. Ibid.
65. Ibid.

Corinthians 13:1. "Though I speak with the tongues of men or of angels ..." Paul communicated the whole, his entire speaking apparatus, by naming only the part, "the tongue." Paul described 275 persons by naming them "souls" in Acts 27:37. Paul also beseeched the Romans to present their "bodies" as living sacrifices.[66] Paul's choice of "body" may underscore the distinction which he draws between the flesh and spirit. Further, his use of the term "body" may imply that the old nature, as in Romans 6, must die to sin in order that the new nature might live unto righteousness.[67]

Merism

A merism occurs when the totality of an entity is communicated by naming two opposite extremes or two contrasting parts. Ephesians 3:18 includes a threefold merism for instance. Paul prayed that the Ephesian believers might know "what is the breadth and length and height and depth" of the love of Christ[68] The Psalmist stated that from the rising of the sun unto its setting the Lord's name is to be praised. The psalmist, of course, did not intend that the praise of the Lord terminate at sundown. Rather, the psalmist wished that the Lord's name be praised at all times.

Euphemism

When a less offensive or less unpleasant entity substitutes for another entity, the figure is a euphemism. In Matthew 1:25, for instance, Matthew records that Joseph did not "know" Mary until Mary gave birth to Christ. In Acts 7:60, Luke records the martyrdom of Stephen by stating that "he fell asleep."[69]

Hendiadys

Hendiadys is a figure of speech that is designed to add emphasis and vividness to a concept by using two terms to express a single concept. Paul in Ephesians 6:18 urged the Ephesian believers to

66. Ibid.
67. Ibid.
68. Ibid.
69. Ibid.

pray "with all prayer and supplication." There are, of course, different nuances to the terms "prayer" and "supplication," but the use of both terms adds vividness and emphasis to Paul's command to pray.[70]

Similarly, there are different nuances to the terms "affection" and "compassion." Paul used both terms in conjunction in Philippians 2:1 for emphasis and vividness—"... if there be any affection and compassion ..."[71]

Hyperbole

Hyberbole is simply an exaggeration for emphasis. "I'm so hungry I could eat a horse" is common hyperbolic figure of speech. In hyperbole, the author's point is overstated more than is literally the reality. Jesus, to emphasize the importance of sanctification, stated in Matthew 5:29–30, "if your right eye makes you stumble, tear it out, and throw it from you ..." Similarly, Paul, to emphasize the necessity and importance of love even though one does great deeds, stated in 1 Corinthians 13:3, "... if I give all my possessions to feed the poor, and if I deliver my body to be burned, but do not have love, it profits me nothing."[72]

Personification

Personification is a figure of speech whereby the author ascribes human attributes to some inanimate or abstract entity. In 1 Corinthians 12:15–16, Paul personified "the foot" in his discussion of the interdependency of Christ's body—"If the foot shall say, because I am not the hand ..." The "foot" though animate, has in and of itself no intelligent capacity. Likewise, Christ in Matthew 6:34 ascribed intelligent attributes to a "day." Christ said "... for tomorrow will care for itself. Each day has enough trouble of its own."[73]

Anthropomorphism and Anthropopathism

70. Ibid.
71. Ibid.
72. Ibid.
73. Ibid.

Anthropomorphism is the figure of speech where God is represented in the form of a human. Anthropopathism is the figure of speech where God is represented as having the attributes of a human. Anthropopathism usually occurs where an author ascribes human emotions to God. Christ used the figure of anthropomorphism in Matthew 18:10—"Their angels do always behold the face of my Father." The Father, of course, does not have a literal human face. Christ used this figure to underscore that God is personal and may be personally known. Forgetting is a human attribute. Luke 12:6 includes the following anthropopathism—"Not one of them is forgotten before God."[74] It is impossible for God to forget. The point of this figure of speech is that God is mindful of his own.

Zoomorphism

Zoopmorphism is the figure of speech where God is represented as having the attributes or form of animals or plants. Christ is the root of Jesse in Isaiah 11:10. Christ as both God and man, the God-man, is represented in the form of a plant—"There shall come the root of Jesse ..." Further, Christ is presented as a "lamb," a kind of animal, in John 1:29.[75] The point of the zoomorphism is that Christ is the sacrifice for the world—"... Behold the Lamb of God who takes away the sin of the world."[76]

Conclusion

Truly, the rhetorical tool of a figure of speech may turn a particular term or phrase into a microcosm of meaning. Not only does the lexical data of a term inform the meaning of the text in which it appears, the rhetorical data capsuled in a figure of speech informs the meaning of a text which nests the figure. The interplay of lexicography and rhetoric composes some of the infinite richness of the Scripture.

74. Ibid.
75. Ibid.
76. Ibid.

2.2C WRITE AN EXEGETICAL OUTLINE

What Is an Exegetical Outline?

An exegetical outline is a list of propositions that mirror the content of a given passage. The aim of the exegetical outline is to restate in a series of propositions what the Holy Spirit put into a text. A good exegetical outline says what the Holy Spirit said the way the Holy Spirit said it. An exegetical outline is the first bridge between exegesis and sermonic development. When the exegete has exegetically outlined a passage, the exegete can develop the exegetical outline into a sermon outline.

But not only the propositions of the exegetical outline must mirror a given text, the propositions' relation to each other in the outline must pattern the text. The subject/complement of the passage must constitute the thesis of the exegetical outline. The major divisions of the passage must constitute the major propositions of the exegetical outline. The sentences within the major divisions of the passage must constitute the subordination propositions of the exegetical outline.[77.] In sum, the exegetical outline and the passage should say essentially the same thing, only in different form.[78]

The Procedure Explained

First Step: Praying for Illumination, Scan the Grammatical Diagram for Syntactical Relationships

The first step of the procedure for exegetical outlining is to pray over the most efficient referent for exegetical outlining, the

---

77. For a comparison with a different approach to sermonic structure, see Walter L. Liefield's excellent *NT Exposition* (Grand Rapids: Zondervan, 1984), 15–133. Another excellent work for comparison is William J. Larkin's *Manual of Greek Exegesis for Preachers* (n.p.: W.J. Larkin, 1987).

78. The following discussion of the exegetical outlining is largely drawn from class lectures from Dallas Theological Seminary's New Testament department. In conservative academia, DTS's course, "204—Exegetical Method in Ephesians" remains the "gold standard" of exegetical courses. Truly, the exegetical method taught in the course, particularly the method for exegetical outlining, is as unique as it is seminal.

grammatical diagram. The diagram is the best referent for developing an exegetical outline because (1) it allows the exegete to view the grammatical relationships of the passage spatially. As the exegete thinks through the passage grammatically, he will be better able to "translate" the grammatical relationships into an outline. (2) If the exegete has followed this method outlined in this treatise, the exegete has identified syntactical relationships and translated figures of speech on the grammatical diagram. Syntax and the meaning of figures of speech form the building blocks of an exegetical outline. (3) The grammatical diagram is the best referent for developing the exegetical outline because the independent and subordinate clauses with their conjunction/connectives are readily visible.

Second Step: Locate the Main Verbs and Other Structural Markers; Connect the Other Structural Markers to the Verbs They Modify

By focusing the independent clauses of the passage the exegete will focus on the gist of the passage. By further focusing the subjects and main verbs of the independent clauses will begin to qualify the gist the passage.

What is a structural marker? Structural markers are terms of such importance in the passage that they provide structural focal points in the author's flow of argument. Structural markers provide the "nerve centers" of the passage. The most important structural markers are main verbs. Three other constructions are always important structural markers: circumstantial (adverbial) participles, adverbial infinitives, and subordinate conjunctions.[79] Circumstantial or adverbial participles are always important structural markers because adverbial participles and the adverbial clauses that often revolve around them provide some of richest expressions in the Greek Testament. Such expressions are similarly important in the Hebrew Testament. Adverbial infinitives are always important in both Hebrew and Greek. In Greek, infinitives tied to prepositions should be treated as a unit, such as infinitives

---

79. Unpublished class notes, "204—Exegetical Method in Ephesians," Dallas Theological Seminary, spring 1988, 2.

of purpose, result, and time. Subordinate conjunctions are always key structural markers in both Hebrew and Greek.

In some passages, less common but sometimes important structural markers appear. A crucial adverbial preposition may be a structural marker if the preposition is central to a passage's flow of argument. A relative pronoun that fits into the syntactical categories of cause, purpose, result, concession, or condition qualifies as a structural marker. Some non-nominative cases where the noun form has an adverbial nuance that is crucial to the passage, such a dative of means or subjective genitive. The three latter forms are only sometimes structural markers; the former four forms, main verbs, circumstantial participles, adverbial infinitives, and subordinate conjunctions are always structural markers.

Third Step: List the Structural Markers, in the Order They Appear, on the Left Side of a Page

A list of the structural markers on the left side of a worksheet will provide the exegete with structural markers for his exegetical outline. Immediately after the structural marker listed on the left side of a worksheet the exegete should identify the syntactical category of the marker and the main verb to which it is connected. Ignore conjunction/connectives that begin a paragraph. These are often called "sign post" connectives; their purpose is to tie paragraphs together. The sign post connectives are crucial in binding paragraphs together but their role in exegetically outlining the interior of a paragraph is minimal.

Fourth Step: Form Propositions from the Structural Markers Using the $z^1{-}x{-}z^2{-}y$ Formula

What is the $z^1{-}x{-}z^2{-}y$ formula? Each structural marker and its attendant phrase or clause (if there is one) provides a subject and a complement. "x" stands for the subject; "y" stands for the complement. The subject, "x", and the complement, "y", for each proposition of the exegetical outline must come from the text. Exegetes trained at Dallas Theological Seminary call the "x" the "unqualified subject" and the "y" the "unqualified complement."

To illustrate the procedure, it may be helpful to start with a sample proposition that would result from using the $z^{1\text{-}}$ x - $z^{2\text{-}}$ y formula. The four elements of the $z^{1\text{-}}$ x - $z^{2\text{-}}$ y formula will be identified within the proposition. Then, the next paragraph will demonstrate how each of the four elements of the proposition came from a given text. The following proposition includes the elements of the $z^{1\text{-}}$ x - $z^{2\text{-}}$ y formula:

The reason exegetes at Greenville Presbyterian Theological Seminary exegete according to a comprehensive procedure is to experience God in an objective, thorough, and life-transforming manner.

The unqualified subject in this sentence is "exegesis according to a comprehensive procedure." The subject of sentence, paragraph, discourse, or book of the Bible answers the question, "What is this passage talking about?" The quotation above is about exegetes' exegeting according to a comprehensive procedure. The central idea is exegetes' exegeting. The complement of a sentence, paragraph, discourse, or book is the answer to the question, "What idea completes the subject?" If the subject performs some action, what action does the subject perform? What does the passage say about the subject? In the quotation above, what does the quotation say about "exegetes' exegeting"? The idea that completes the subject is the "experience of God in an objective, thorough, and life-transforming manner." The subject/complement or the "x"/"y" compose substantive elements of the formula. Thus, a proposition designed according to this formula would have a subject and predicate substantially derived from the passage. While the "x" and "y" are substantive elements, the two elements "z" elements are syntactical elements. The "z^1" and "z^2" serve to connect the subject with the complement according to the syntactical use in the passage. The "z^1" is the syntactical category of the complement; "z^2" is any "to be" verb that connects the subject, "x", with its complement, "y".

The proposition above derived the four elements of the $z^{1\text{-}}$ x - $z^{2\text{-}}$ y formula from an original text. An original text from which the proposition above may have been derived is as follows:

So then it comes to pass, that exegetes in and around Greenville Presbyterian Theological Seminary are busy exegeting according to a very thorough exegetical procedure almost all the time, including breaks between classes, in order that they might experience God in an objective, thorough, and life-changing manner.

First, the "so then it came to pass" is a connective signpost. It serves little function in the interior of the paragraph above; it does, however, serve a significant function in connecting this paragraph to the one that proceeded it. This connective indicates an historical paragraph breaks into the author's flow of discussion. For the purpose of exegetical outlining, as stated *infra*, connectives such as this one may be omitted. The exegete should make a list of the structural markers in the passage. In the hypothetical original passage above, the structural markers are as follows:

"were exegeting" (main verb of an independent clause)

"that ... [they might experience]" (subordinate conjunction introducing a purpose or reason clause)

The main verb of the hypothetical passage above is "were exegeting." The main verb may serve as the "x" or subject of a z^1-x-z^2-y proposition. The exegete may begin with z^1-"exegetes were exegeting"-z^2-y. The exegete may then take the second structural marker, the "that" (in Greek this would be a *hina*). The second structural maker may serve as the "y" or complement. Thus, the exegete may continue with the complement of the formula: z^1-"exegetes were exegeting"-z^2-"might experience ..." The syntactical category of this subordinate clause is purpose or reason. The reason may serve as the z^1 syntactical element of the formula. The exegete may insert "the reason"—"exegetes were exegeting"-"z^2"-"might experience ..." Finally, the z^2 may simply be a connecting "to be" verb to bind the subject "x" and complement "y". The z^1-x-z^2-y proposition would therefore be "the reason exegetes at Greeneville Presbyterian Theological Seminary exegete continually according to a comprehensive procedure was to experience God in an objective, thorough, and life-changing manner.[80]

Using the list of structural markers, the exegete should continue to design z^1-x-z^2-y propositions. The exegete should take the structural markers in pairs, choosing the first to be the subject "x" and the second to be the complement "y". The syntactical category of the complement "y" will serve as the "z^1".[81]

The exegete may consider the propositions listed in Philippians 1:9–11:

> [1:9] The content (z^1) of Paul's prayer (x) is that (z^2) the Philippians' might abound in love in knowledge and all discernment (y).
>
> [1:10a] The purpose (z^1) of abounding love (x) is that (z^2) the Philippians might discern the more excellent things (y).
>
> [1:10b] The result (z^1) of discerning more excellent things (x) is (z^2) the Philippians will be pure and blameless in the day of Christ (y).
>
> [1:11a] The reason (z^1) the Philippians are pure and blameless (x) is because (z^2) they are filled with the fruit of righteousness that comes through Christ (y).
>
> [1:11b] The result (z^1) of the Philippians' being pure and blameless in the day of Christ (x) is that (z^2) there will be praise and glory to God (y).[82]

Final Step: Group the Propositions Together into an Outline

At this point, the exegete has a list of propositions around the structural markers in the passage. The exegete can now take the propositions and evaluate each proposition's scope. The exegete can use the list of propositions to form an outline in the following two ways: (1) the exegete can take propositions which have similar content and group them into a single proposition composed of the

80. Ibid.
81. Ibid.
82. Ibid.

"biggest" subject and the "biggest" complement. The subject "x" which has the widest scope and the complement "y" which has the widest scope form a broader proposition which can serve as a Roman numeral of the outline. (2) The exegete can also evaluate the scope of each proposition. If an earlier proposition is broad enough to include later ones the exegete could use the broad proposition as the Roman numeral and the later ones as the subordinate points. Suppose the passage has five propositions, "A", "B", "C", "D", and "E". Suppose "A" and "B" have similar content "C" is broad enough to include "D" and "E". The exegete could group the broadest subject "x" of "A" and "B" with the broadest complement "y" or "A" and "B" into a single proposition. This merged proposition could serve as Roman numeral "I" for the outline. Propositions "A" and "B" could serve as the subordinate points "A" and "B" under Roman numeral "I". Since "C" is broad enough to include both "D" and "E", "C" could serve as Roman numeral "II" and "D" with "E" could serve as two subordinate points, "A" and "B", under Roman numeral "II". To arrive at the exegetical subject/complement of the passage, the exegete can merge Roman numeral "I" and "II" into a single proposition. This single proposition is the overall exegetical idea of the passage.[83]

The grouping of propositions by either (1) merging or (2) subordinating discussed above issues from the exegete's discretion. There is no perfect exegetical outline; there is no infallible way to apply the z^1-x-z^2-y formula and group the propositions. The goal of the z^1-x-z^2-y formula and the exegetical outline is to reflect the thought of the author of the passage of Scripture.[84]

The exegete may consider the following treatment of Philippians 1:9–11 as an example of exegetical outlining. The exegete may compare the outline with the Greek text of Philippians 1:9–11.

I. [1:9–10] The result (z^1) of abounding love for which Paul prays (x) is (z^2) the Philippians' being pure and blameless in the day of Christ (y).

83. Ibid.
84. Ibid.

A. [1:9] The content (z^1) of Paul's prayer (x) is that (z^2) the Phillipians' might abound in love in knowledge and all discernment (y).

B. [1:10a] The purpose (z^1) of abounding love (x) is that (z^2) the Philippians might discern the more excellent things (y).

C. [1:10b] The result (z^1) of discerning more excellent things (x) is (z^2) the Philippians will be pure and blameless in the day of Christ (y).

II. [1:11] The result (z^1) of the Philippians being pure and blameless in the day of Christ (x) is (z^2) praise and glory to God (y).

A. [1:11a] The reason (z^1) the Philippians are pure and blameless (x) is because (z^2) they are filled with the fruit of righteousnes that comes through Christ (y).

B. [1:11b] The result (z^1) of the Philippians' being pure and blameless in the day of Christ (x) is that (z^2) there will be praise and glory to God (y).[85]

2.2D Determine the Paragraph's Subject/Complement

A Guide to Determine the Paragraph's Subject

At this point in the process the exegete should have such a wealth of material that the central idea of the passage is clear to him. The following list of questions may help in finding the paragraph's subject:

1. What is the passage talking about?
2. What is the passage not talking about, i.e., what are its limits?
3. What key ideas does the passage include?
4. What terms, phrases, or images relate repeated concepts?

85. Ibid.

5. What phrase most accurately circumscribes the text without excluding anything in it or adding anything to it?

A Guide to Determine the Paragraph's Complement

The following list of questions may help in finding the paragraph's complement:

1. What does the passage say about its central idea, its subject?
2. What idea does the passage add to its subject?
3. How does the passage interpret itself?
4. How does the passage interpret its complement?

Adding the passage's subject and complement together into a single sentence provides its thesis—the whole of the text subsumed in one succinct but thorough sentence. The exegete may use a dictionary or a thesaurus to hammer out the most accurate and understandable thesis that he can. The final version of this homiletic thesis provides a frame for all that the exegete does and says from the pulpit.

Upon completion of the exegetical outline, the exegetical subject/complement may be more readily discernible: Paul's prayer for the Philippians (subject) is for an abounding love that results in purity at the believer's judgment and the praise and glory of God (complement).

2.2G MAKE A LIST OF INTERPRETATIVE QUESTIONS ON THE PASSAGE, PUT THEM IN LOGICAL ORDER, AND ANSWER THEM BY WHATEVER TECHNIQUE OR TOOL NECESSARY, INCLUDING THE KEY EXEGETICAL COMMENTARIES

Make a List of Interpretative Questions

Asking the Right Questions in the Right Order Is the Essence of Good Bible Study

Howard Hendricks of Dallas Theological Seminary, in his outstanding course on Hermeneutics and Bible Study Methods, summarized the procedure for Bible study in the following sentence: "good Bible study is asking the text the right questions in the right order." Any text read or heard should spar questions. The questions may follow the standard "who?", "what?", "when?", "where?", "why?", and "how?" patterns. Or, questions about a text may be fact specific, such as "Why this word order?" or "How is this term used in other parts of this book, other writings of this author, or the entire Testament?" While gaining a book background and overview as in 2.1 and exploring a paragraph as in 2.2, questions should "leap off the page." If questions that hearers have about the text are not answered in the sermon or lecture, the expositor has not done his job. Hearers want their questions answered.

A Formula for Asking Exegetical Questions:
Interrogative-Text-Function

The following formula may assist the exegete in forming a list of exegetical questions. Exegetical questions are questions which the text alone can answer. For instance, "why does the text order its three direct objects in the order that it does?" Or, "how does this purpose clause of the text differ from the previous purpose clause?" In the formula for asking exegetical questions, the text or some portion of the text is the question's subject. The formula is "interrogative-text-function." (1) The first component of the formula is "interrogative." The standard "who?", "what?", "when?", "where?", "why?", and "how?" serve as the interrogatives which commonly construct questions in the English language. (2) The second component of the formula is the "text." This means the text or any part or parts of the text. For instance, the exegete may ask "how does this list of nouns in the text differ from a similar list of nouns the author uses in another book of the Bible?" The interrogative is "how." The "text" portion is a noun list. (3) The third component of the formula is "function." The function component is some role the text serves or portion of the text serves. For instance, "why does this imperative differ only slightly from the previous imperative?" The interrogative is "why." The text portion is a particular imperative. The function component is the differing role that the particular imperative plays in contradistinction to the previous imperative. Another example of the function component is as follows: "How does the introduction of the text function to 'set the stage' for what follows?" The interrogative is "how." The text component is the text's introduction. The function component is setting the stage or introducing what follows.

A Formula for Asking Homiletic Questions

While the focus of exegetical questions is on the text, that is, what does the text say, the focus of homiletic questions is on the expositor. Homiletic questions are summed by the following question: "How may I, as a faithful expositor, communicate this text or any of its parts?" Homiletic questions fall into the five categories of the rhetorical processes: (1) Explanatory: "How may I explain this?" (2) Illustrative: "How may I illustrate this?" (3) Argumentative: "How may I persuade my hearers to believe or do this?" (4) Exhortative: "How can I encourage my hearers to believe or do this?" (5) Applicatory: "How may I apply this to my hearers?" In each of these five homiletic categories of questions, hearers ask a corresponding question of the expositor. Corresponding hearers questions include: (1) Explanatory: "Expositor, would you please explain this to me?" (2) Illustrative: "Expositor, would you please give me an illustration so I can understand what this means?" (3) Argumentative: "Expositor, I'm not sure if I buy this; so would you convince me?" (4) Exhortative: "Expositor, I can see what your saying but I'm discouraged; would you encourage me?" (5) Applicatory: "How does this look in real life? How does this change life in the real world?"

Put the Interpretative Questions into a Logical Order

Much more important than the order of the questions is the content of the questions. But once the expositor has formulated the exegetical and homiletic questions, he should proceed to order them. The reasons for ordering the questions are twofold. (1) An orderly progression of questions will help the expositor remember the course of his study. Good exegesis must be remembered in order to be communicated. (2) An orderly progression of questions will allow later questions to build on the material of earlier questions. There are several ways to order the questions once they are drafted. The most logical order of the questions may be the order they appear in the text. Another ordering principle may be kind. The expositor may order all questions relating to terms together, questions relating to grammar, questions relating to background data, or questions relating to theology together. The advantage of this ordering principle is that the expositor will probably be using the same tools to "dig" for answers; thus it may be more efficient to be using the lexicons at the same time or systematic theologies at the same time and so forth. Whether by "textual order" or "tool order," the expositor should order the questions logically by either or both principles. The whole point of ordering the questions is to make the Bible study more orderly and efficient.

Answer the Interpretative Questions by Whatever Technique or Tool Necessary

Answering exegetical and homiletic questions is the difference between good preaching and bad preaching. Good preachers answer their hearers' questions. When hearers look at the text that the preacher read, they have questions they expect the preacher to answer. Under good preaching, the hearer may leave the sermon and say "I learned this, and this, and so forth." A text poses questions; a hearer's exposure to the text poses questions. The preacher who does not answer these questions is negligent, having violated his duty of care.

This thesis has by now introduced the exegete to a variety of exegetical tools. Familiarity with and ability to use them is imperative. By practice the exegete may become proficient at using the lexicons, grammars, concordances, and exegetical commentaries available. The exegetical questions and the homiletic questions that issue from the exegesis of the passage must be answered using primary sources and secondary sources. Primary sources are tools that let the exegete "dig" for himself; they include lexicons, grammars, and concordances. Secondary sources include tools where the exegesis is already done for the exegete, as in exegetical commentaries. It is best that the exegete use the primary sources first because (1) they allow the exegete to experience the joy of personal discovery and (2) they give the exegete a base to approach the exegetical commentaries with a critical and "open eye" mind set.

Consult the Key Exegetical Commentaries

The skillful exegete must be aware of the key exegetical commentaries. These are helps to verify the accuracy of his interpretations, sources of new exegetical observations, and evaluations of differing interpretative options.

For a fuller examination of various exegetical commentaries, one may purchase *Bibliography for Old Testament Exegesis and Exposition*, compiled by Kenneth L. Barker, Bruce K. Waltke, and Roy B. Zuck of Dallas Theological Seminary.[86] A more recent annotated commentary list has been compiled by the Old Testament faculty of Dallas Seminary, *An Annotated Bibliography for the Study of the Old Testament*.[87] Similarly, there is a comparable New Testament bibliography compiled by S. Louis Johnson, professor emeritus of Dallas Seminary, *Bibliography for New Testament Exegesis and Exposition*.[88]

The following is a list of outstanding exegetical commentaries on each book of the Bible. The criteria for choosing the following is linguistic accuracy; the following is not an endorsement of all theology and all particular conclusions of the commentators. The commentators who hold to biblical inerrancy are marked with an asterisk (*). When reading liberals, the following guidelines

---

86. Kenneth L. Barker, Bruce K. Waltke, and Roy B. Zuck, *Bibliography for Old Testament Exegesis and Exposition* (Dallas: Dallas Seminary, 1979), available from Dallas Seminary Campus Bookstore.

87. The Department of Semitics and Old Testament Studies, *An Annotated Bibliography for the Study of the Old Testament* (unpublished, April 1985), available from Dallas Seminary Campus Bookstore.

88. S. Louis Johnson, *Bibliography for New Testament Exegesis and Exposition* (unpublished), available from the Dallas Seminary Campus Bookstore.

are suggested: (1) View dates critically. (2) Gloss over or skip speculation about sources. (3) Focus on Greek quotations, Hebrew quotations, Scripture references or verse lists, or discussions of background material, such as archeological and cultural data. Background material must also be reviewed critically. Late in the exegetical process, as in phase "3" and "4," the exegete should consult the Puritan commentaries. The focus in the following commentary list is linguistic, lexical, and exegetical.

Old Testament Exegetical/Expositional Commentaries (in a proposed order of exegetical usefulness):

Genesis

*Bush, George. *Notes on Genesis*.

*Candlish, Robert. *Genesis*.

Cassuto, Umberto. *A Commentary on the Book of Genesis*.

*Ross, Allen. *Genesis*.

*Kidner, Derek. *Genesis*.

Wenham, G. J. *The Book of Genesis*.

Westermann, Claus. *Genesis 1–11, A Commentary*.

Exodus

Jacobs, B. *Exodus: The Second Book of the Law*.

Childs, Brevard. *The Book of Exodus: A Critical Theological Commentary*.

Cassuto, Umberto. *A Commentary on the Book of Exodus*.

*Cole, Alan. *Exodus*.

Driver, S.R. *The Book of Exodus*.

* The commentators who hold to biblical inerrancy

Leviticus

Wenham, G.J. *The Book of Leviticus.*
Harrison, R.K. *Leviticus: An Introduction and Commentary.*[89]
Noth, Martin. *Leviticus.*
Bamberger, B.J. *Leviticus.*
*Bonar, A.A. *A Commentary on Leviticus.*

Numbers

Harrison, R.K. *An Exegetical Commentary: Numbers.*
*Keil, C.F., and F. Delitzch. *Biblical Commentary on the Old Testament.*
Wenham, G.J. *Numbers: An Introduction and Commentary.*
Budd, Philip J. *Word Biblical Commentary: Numbers.*
Snaith, N.H. *Numbers: New Century Bible Commentary.*
Honeycutt, Roy Lee. *Leviticus, Numbers, Deuteronomy.*

Deuteronomy

*Craigie, P.C. *The Book of Deuteronomy.*
*Thompson, J. A. *Deuteronomy.*
Driver, S. R. *A Critical and Exegetical Commentary on Deuteronomy.*
*Kline, M. G. *The Treaty of the Great King: The Covenant Structure of Deuteronomy: Studies and Commentary.*
Clements, R. E. *God's Chosen People.*

---

* The commentators who hold to biblical inerrancy

89. Harrison is not listed as an inerrancist because he holds to the existence of a pre-Adamic humanoid race.

Joshua

Boling, Robert G. *Joshua. The Anchor Bible.*

Butler, Trent C. *Word Biblical Commentary: Joshua.*

Judges

Boling, Robert G. *Judges.*

*Cundall, Arthur E. *Judges.*

Soggin, J. Albert. *Judges.*

Burney, C.G. *The Book of Judges with Introduction and Notes.*

Ruth

*Cundall, Arthur E. and Leon Morris. *Tyndale Old Testament Commentaries: Ruth.*

Campbell, Edward F. *Ruth. Anchor Bible.*

Jouon, P. Paul. *Ruth, Commentaire Philologique et exegetique.*

Halls, Ronald M. *The Theology of the Book of Ruth.*

Samuel

*Chafin, Kenneth L. *1 and 2 Samuel. Communicator's Commentary.*

Klein, Ralph W. *Word Biblical Commentary. 1 Samuel*

McCarter, P. Kyle. *1 Samuel. The Anchor Bible.*

Driver, S. R. *Notes on the Hebrew Text and the Topography of the Books of Samuel.*

Payne, David F. *1 and 2 Samuel.*

Ackroyd, Peter R. *The Second Book of Samuel.*

Kings

*Dilday, Russell H. *1 and 2 Kings: Communicators Commentary.*

* The commentators who hold to biblical inerrancy

Jones, G. H. *1 and 2 Kings*.

Mongonery, James A. and H. S. Gehman. *A Critical and Exegetical Commentary on the Books of Kings*.

Long, Burke O. *1 Kings, with an Introduction to Historical Literature. The Forms of the Old Testament Literature*.

Chronicles

Williamson, H. G. M. *1 and 2 Chronicles*.

Meyers, Jacob M. *1 Chronicles [2 Chronicles]: A New Translation with Introduction and Commentary*.

Japhet, Sara. *The Ideology of the Book of Chronicles and Its Place in Biblical Thought*.

*Dillard, Ray. *2 Chronicles. Word Biblical Commentary*.

Ezra-Nehemiah

Fensham, F. Charles. *The Books of Ezra and Nehemiah*.

Myers, Jacob M. *Ezra-Nehemiah. The Anchor Bible*.

*Campbell, Donald K. *Nehemiah: Man in Charge*.

Esther

Moore, C. A. *Esther*

Job

Rowley, Harold H. *The Book of Job*.

Pope, Marvin H. *Job. Introduction Translation and Notes*.

Habel, Norman. *The Book of Job: A Commentary*.

*Andersen, Francis I. *Job: An Introduction and Commentary*.

*Zuck, Roy, ed. *Sitting with Job*.

---

* The commentators who hold to biblical inerrancy

Psalms

Kirkpatrick, A. F. *The Book of Psalms. The Cambridge Bible for Schools and Colleges.*

Anderson, A. A. *The Book of Psalms.*

*Perowne, J. J. Stewart. *The Book of Psalms.*

*Delitzsch, Fanz. *Biblical Commentary on the Psalms.*

Craigie, Peter C., Marvin E. Tate, and Leslie C. Allen. *Psalms 1–50, Psalms 51–100, Psalms 101–150. Word Biblical Commentary.*

Proverbs

Delitzsch, Franz. *Biblical Commentary on the Proverbs of Solomon.*

*Kidner, Derek. *The Proverbs: An Introduction and Commentary.*

Cohen, A. *Proverbs: Hebrew Text and English Translation with an Introduction and Commentary.*

Ecclesiastes

Ginsburg, Christian D. *The Song of Songs and Qoheleth.*

*Eaton, Michael A. *Ecclesiastes, an Introduction and Commentary.*

Song of Solomon

*Glickman, S. Craig. *A Song for Lovers.*

Delitzsch, Franz. *Commentary on the Song of Songs and Ecclesiastes.*

*Carr, Lloyd. *The Song of Solomon.*

Falk, Marcia. *Love Lyrics from the Bible: A Translation and Literary Study of the Song of Songs.*

* The commentators who hold to biblical inerrancy

Landy, Francis. *Paradoxes of Paradise: Identity and Differences in the Song of Songs*.

Pope, M. H. *Song of Songs*.

Isaiah

*Young, Edward J. *The Book of Isaiah. New International Commentary on the Old Testament*.

Leupold, H.C. *Isaiah*.

North, Christopher R. *The Second Isaiah*.

Gray, G. B. *A Critical and Exegetical Commentary on the Book of Isaiah, I–XXVII*

Gitay, Yehoshua. *Prophecy and Persuasion. A Study of Isaiah 40–48. Forum Theologiae Linguisticae*.

Jeremiah

Bright, John. *Jeremiah: A New Translation with Introduction and Commentary. Anchor Bible*.

Holladay, William. *Jeremiah. Hermeneia*.

*Thompson, John A. *The Book of Jeremiah*.

*Peterson, Eugene. *Run with the Horses*.

Lamentations

Hillers, Delbert. *Lamentations: A New Translation with Introduction and Commentary. Anchor Bible*.

Roberts, J. M. *Lamentations. Hermeneia*.

*Laetsch, Theo. *Jeremiah*.

Albrektson, Bertil. *Studies in the Text and Theology of the Book of Lamentations*.

Gottwald, Norman K. *Studies in the Book of Lamentations*.

* The commentators who hold to biblical inerrancy

Ezekiel

Zimmerli, Walther. *A Commentary on the Book of the Prophet Ezekiel, Chapters 1–24; A Commentary on the Book of the Prophet Ezekiel, Chapters 25–48.*

Greenberg, Moshe. *The Anchor Bible. Ezekiel 1–20.*

*Taylor, John B. *Ezekiel: An Introduction and Commentary.*

Eichrodt, Walther. *Ezekiel: A Commentary.*

Daniel

Montgomery, James A. *A Critical and Exegetical Commentary on the Book of Daniel.*

*Baldwin, Joyce G. *Daniel, and Introduction and Commentary.*

Wiseman, D. J. Mitchell, T. C., et. al. *Notes on Some Problems in the Book of Daniel.*

Young, E.D. *Daniel.*

Leupold, H. C. *Daniel.*

Campbell, Donald K. *Daniel: Decoder of Dreams.*

Hosea

Wolff, Hans Walter. *Hosea. Hermeneia.*

*Chisholm, Robert B., Jr. *Minor Prophets.*

*McComiskey, Thomas E. *The Minor Prophets: An Exegetical and Expositional Commentary.*

Mays, James Luther. *Hosea. Old Testament Library.*

Stuart, Douglas. *Hosea-Jonah. Word Biblical Commentary.*

Harper, William Rainey. *A Critical and Exegetical Commentary on Amos and Hosea.*

Kidner, Derek. *Love to the Loveless: The Message of Hosea.*

---

* The commentators who hold to biblical inerrancy

Joel

Wolff, Hans W. *Joel and Amos. Hermeneia.*

*Dillard, Ray. *The Minor Prophets: An Exegetical and Expostional Commentary.*

*Chisholm, Robert B., Jr. *Minor Prophets.*

*Finley, Thomas J. *Wycliffe Exegetical Commentary.*

Allen, Leslie C. *The Books of Joel, Obadiah, Jonah, and Micah. New International Commentary.*

Kapelrud, Arvid S. *Joel Studies.*

Amos

Mays, James L. *Amos: A Commentary. Old Testament Library.*

Wolf, Hans W. *Joel and Amos.*

*Chisholm, Robert B., Jr. *Minor Prophets.*

*Neuhaus, Jeffrey. *The Minor Prophets: An Exegetical and Expositional Commentary.*

*Finley, Thomas J. *Wycliffe Exegetical Commentary.*

Cripps, Richard S. *A Critical and Exegetical Commentary on the Book of Amos.*

Anderson, Francis I. and David N. Freedman. *Amos. Anchor Bible.*

Harper, William R. *A Critical and Exegetical Commentary on Amos and Hosea.*

DeWaard, J. and Smalley, William A. *A Translator's Handbook on the Book of Amos.*

Obadiah

Watts, John D. W. *Obadiah: A Critical and Exegetical Commentary.*

* The commentators who hold to biblical inerrancy

*Chisholm, Robert B., Jr. *Minor Prophets*.

*Finley, Thomas J. *Wycliffe Exegetical Commentary*.

Allen, Leslie C. *The Books of Joel, Obadiah, Jonah, and Micah*. New International Commentary.

Jonah

*Chisholm, Robert B., Jr. *Minor Prophets*.

Allen, Leslie C. *The Books of Joel, Obadiah, Jonah, and Micah*. New International Commentary.

Stuart, Douglas. *Hosea-Jonah*. Word Biblical Commentary.

Micah

*Chisholm, Robert B., Jr. *Minor Prophets*.

Allen, Leslie C. *The Books of Joel, Obadiah, Jonah, and Micah*. New International Commentary.

Hillers. *Micah*. Hermeneia.

Nahum

*Maier, Walther A. *The Book of Nahum*.

*Chisholm, Robert B., Jr. *Minor Prophets*.

Smith, Ralph L. *Micah-Malachi*. Word Biblical Commentary.

Habakkuk

Gowan, Donald E. *The Triumph of Faith in Habakkuk*.

*Chisholm, Robert B., Jr. *Minor Prophets*.

Smith, Ralph L. *Micah-Malachi*. Word Biblical Commentary.

Zephaniah

*Chisholm, Robert B., Jr. *Minor Prophets*.

* The commentators who hold to biblical inerrancy

Smith, Ralph L. *Micah-Malachi. Word Biblical Commentary.*

Kapelrud, Arvid S. *The Prophet Zephaniah: Morphology and Ideas.*

Haggai

Pusey, E. B. *The Minor Prophets: A Commentary.*
*Chisholm, Robert B., Jr. *Minor Prophets.*
*Baldwin, Joyce. *Haggai, Zechariah, Malachi.*
Smith, Ralph L. *Micah-Malachi. Word Biblical Commentary.*
Smith, George Adam. *The Book of the Twelve Prophets.*

Zechariah

*Chisholm, Robert B., Jr. *Minor Prophets.*
Smith, Ralph L. *Micah-Malachi. Word Biblical Commentary.*
*Baldwin, Joyce. *Haggai, Zechariah, Malachi.*
*Unger, Merrill F. *Zechariah: Prophet of Messiah's Glory.*

Malachi

Glazier-McDonald, Beth. *The Divine Messenger.*
*Kaiser, Walter C., Jr. *Malachi: God's Unchanging Love.*
Smith, Ralph L. *Micah-Malachi. Word Commentary.*
*Chisholm, Robert B., Jr. *Minor Prophets.*
Verheof. *Haggai and Malachi. New International Commentary.*
*Baldwin, Joyce. *Haggai, Zechariah, Malachi.*

---

* The commentators who hold to biblical inerrancy

New Testament Exegetical/Expositional Commentaries (in a proposed order of exegetical usefulness:

Matthew

>Bruner, Frederick Dale. *Matthew 1-12. Word Biblical Commentary.*
>
>McNeile. *Matthew.*
>
>Gundry. *Matthew Literary and Theological Art.*

Mark

>Cranfield, C. E. B. *Mark. The New International Critical Commentary.*
>
>Lane, William. *Mark. New International Commentary.*
>
>Tayler. *Mark.*
>
>Swete. *Mark.*

Luke

>Fitzmeyer. *Luke.*
>
>Marshal, I. H. *Luke. New International Greek Testament Commentary.*
>
>*Plumer. *Luke. International Critical Commentary.*
>
>*Godet. *Mark.*

John

>Brown, Raymond. *John. The Anchor Bible.*
>
>Schnackenburg. *John.*
>
>Barret, C. K. *John.*
>
>*Morris, Leon. *John.*
>
>Westcott. *John.*
>
>Lindars. *John.*
>
>* The commentators who hold to biblical inerrancy

Acts

Bruce, F. F. *Acts. New International Commentary on the New Testament*

Marshal, I. H. *Acts. Tyndale New Testament.*

Haenchen. *Acts.*

Longnecker. *Expositors' Bible Commentary.* Vol. 9.

Romans

Cranfield, C. E. B. *Romans. The New International Critical Commentary.*

Sanday-Headlam. *Romans. International Critical Commentary.*

Dunn, James. *Romans. Word Biblical Commentary.*

*Murray, John. *Romans. New International Commentary on the New Testament.*

*Hodge, Charles. *Romans.*

*Morris, Leon. *Romans.*

1 Corinthians

*Plumer. Robertson. *1 Corinthians. International Critical Commentary.*

*Godet. *1 Corinthians.*

2 Corinthians

*Hughes, Philp Edgecomb. *2 Corinthians. New International Commentary on the New Testament.*[90]

Furish. *2 Corinthians. The Anchor Bible.*

Martin, Ralph. *2 Corinthians. Word Biblical Commentary.*

* The commentators who hold to biblical inerrancy

90. Hughes changed his views in later life regarding the biblical doctrine of hell. He left the historic orthodox position by embracing annihilationism. His position at the time of writing his commentaries on 2 Corinthians and Hebrews, however, was orthodox.

Barret, C. K. *2 Corinthians.*

*Plumer. *2 Corinthians. International Critical Commentary.*

Galatians

*Bruce, F. F. *Galatians.*

*Eadie, John. *Galatians, Ephesians, Colossians, Philippians, Thessalonians.*

*Ellicot. *Galatians, Ephesians, Colossians, 1 and 2 Timothy.*

*Burton. *Galatians. International Critical Commentary.*

Betz, Hans Dieter. *Galatians. Hermeneia.*

Ephesians

Barth, Markus. *Ephesians. The Anchor Bible.*

*Robinson. *Ephesians.*

Abbot. *International Critical Commentary.*

Bruce, F. F. *Ephesians, Colossians, Philemon. New International Commentary.*

*Eadie, John. *Galatians, Ephesians, Colossians, Philippians. Thessalonians.*

*Ellicot. *Galatians, Ephesians, Colossians, 1 and 2 Timothy.*

Philippians

Hawthorne, Gerald. *Philippians. Word Biblical Commentary.*

Collange. *Philippians.*

*Eadie, John. *Galatians, Ephesians, Colossians, Philippians, Thessalonians.*

Colossians

Lohse. *Colossians and Philemon. Hermeneia.*

* The commentators who hold to biblical inerrancy

O'Brien, Peter. *Colossians and Philemon. Word Biblical Commentary.*

*Eadie, John. *Galatians, Ephesians, Colossians, Philippians, Thessalonians.*

*Ellicot. *Galatians, Ephesians, Colossians, 1 and 2 Timothy.*

Philemon

Lohse. *Colossians and Philemon. Hermeneia.*

O'Brien, Peter. *Colossians and Philemon. Word Biblical Commentary.*

Martin, Ralph. *Colossians and Philemon. New Century Bible Commentary.*

*Moule. *Colossians and Philemon.*

1 and 2 Thessalonians

*Hiebert. *1 and 2 Thessalonians.*

Bruce, F. F. *1 and 2 Thessalonians. Word Biblical Commentary.*

*Lenski. *1 and 2 Thessalonians.*

*Eadie, John. *Galatians, Ephesians, Colossians, Philippians, Thessalonians.*

*Morris, Leon. *1 and 2 Thessalonians. New International Commentary on the New Testament.*

1 and 2 Timothy

*Lenski. *1 and 2 Timothy.*

Titus

*Ellicot. *Galatians, Ephesians, Colossians, 1 and 2 Timothy.*

*Fee, Gordon. *Pastoral Epistles. Harper New Testament Commentary.*

* The commentators who hold to biblical inerrancy

*Kelly, J. N. D. *The Pastoral Epistles.* Harper New Testament Commentary.

Bernard. *Pastorals.*

Titus

*Kelly, J. N. D. *The Pastoral Epistles.* Harper New Testament Commentary.

Fee, Gordon. *Pastoral Epistles.* Harper New Testament Commentary.

Bernard. *Pastorals.*

Hebrews

Bruce, F. F. Hebrews. *New International Commentary of the NT.*

*Hughes, Philip Edgecomb. *Hebrews.*

Guthrie. *Hebrews. Tyndale New Testament Commentary.*

Westcott. *Hebrews.*

*Owen, John. *Hebrews.*

James

Davids. *James. New International Greek Testament Commentary.*

*Hiebert. *James.*

*Mayor. *James.*

Laws, Sophie. *James.*

1 Peter

*Selwyn. *1 Peter.*

Michaels. *1 Peter. Word Biblical Commentary.*

*Kelley, J. N. D. *Peter and Jude.*

Bigg. Peter and Jude.

* The commentators who hold to biblical inerrancy

2 Peter

    Bauckham. 2 Peter. *Word Biblical Commentary.*

1, 2, and 3 John

    Smalley. *1, 2, and 3 John. Word Biblical Commentary.*

    Brown, Raymond. *1, 2, and 3 John. The Anchor Bible.*

    Marshall, I. H. *1, 2, and 3 John.*

Jude

    *Kelley, J. N. D. *Peter and Jude.*

    Bigg. *Peter and Jude.*

Revelation

    *Swete. *Revelation.*

    *Beale. *Revelation.*

    Mounce, Robert. *Revelation.*

    R. H. Charles. *Revelation. International Critical Commentary.*

    Beasely-Murray. Revelation. *New Century Bible Commentary.*

Converting an Exegetical Outline into an Expositional Outline

What Is the Difference between an Exegetical Outline and an Expositional Outline?

Exegesis occurs in the exegete's study; exposition occurs in the exegete's pulpit and lecturn. An exegetical outline seeks to mirror the content of the paragraph as much as possible. In the preceding outline, for instance, propositions are "time bound," that is, propositions include the historical referents of the text. The outline includes the Apostle Paul who offered the prayer and the historical referents for whom Paul prayed. The expositional outline keeps the

---

* The commentators who hold to biblical inerrancy

concepts of each proposition, but leaves the time bound elements. What remains of each proposition is preachable to any Christian of any era and any circumstance. An expositional outline is therefore universally preachable and teachable. An expositional outline is essentially an exegetical outline whose propositions have been converted into timeless truths. An exegetical outline is merely a sound bridge to the expositional outline. The exegetical outline, although a stepping stone to a preachable expositional outline, is still necessary in the exegete's sermon development because the exegetical outline forces the exegete to rigidly adhere to the text's contour. Departure from the context of the text is the essence of the weakness that plagues the modern evangelical church. Because the exegetical outline is historically bound, it lacks "preachability." The exegete may consider the following conversion of the preceding exegetical outline into an expositional outline.

The "Converted" Exegetical Outline into a Preachable and Teachable Expositional Outline

Expositional thesis: Christians should pray for each other (converted subject) so that their love may abound and produce purity which climaxes on Christians' judgment to the glory of God.

I. [1:9–10] Christians should pray (x) that their love grows into purity and blamelessness on the day of Christ (y).

  A. [1:9] Christians should pray (x) that their love abounds in knowledge and all discernment (y).

  B. [1:10a] Christians should pray (x) that their love might abound to the end they may discern the more excellent things (y).

  C. [1:10b] Discerning the more excellent things (x) results in purity and blamelessness on the day of Christ (y).

II. [1:11] Christians being pure and blameless on the day of Christ (x) will glorify God (y).

A. [1:11a] Christians may be pure and blameless (x) if they are filled with the fruit of righteousness that comes through Christ (y).

B. [1:11b] Christians being pure and blameless in the day of Christ (x) will be praise and glory to God (y).[91]

Converting an Expositional Outline into a Homiletic Outline

The Difference between an Expositional Outline and a Homiletic Outline

A homiletic outline is another developmental step from exegesis into sermonic development. A homiletic outline is simply an expositional outline reordered logically; the essential content is the same. Only order and, if necessary, phraseology is changed. The exegete may find that reordering the material in an expositional outline may improve the communication of the passage's content to his hearers. Further, the exegete may find that "streamlining" some phraseology would improve the sermon's "punch." Altering phraseology for rhetorical effect without altering the essential content of the expositional outline is the goal of writing a homiletic outline. If the exegete finds that the phraseology and order of the expositional outline are adequately "preachable," the exegete is free, of course, not to develop a homiletic outline.

More specifically, in developing the logical order of the homiletic outline, the exegete should insert transitions into the outline. Transitions can consist of any clear means of bridging the propositions. The exegete may first try to bridge the gap between propositions by asking the key logical questions: "when," "where," "why," "how," "what," and "so what." Later, the exegete may develop the conceptual bridges between propositions with illustrations or biblical data from other passages.

---

91. Unpublished class notes, "204—Exegetical Method in Ephesians," Dallas Theological Seminary, Spring '88.

An Example of "Converting" an Expositional Outline into a Homiletic Outline

Homiletic thesis: Pray (converted subject) that love engulfs us, purifies us, and glorifies our God (converted compliment).

I. [1:9–10] Pray (x) that love engulfs us and purifies us until the day of Christ (y).

   [transition: What must our love produce?]

   A. [1:9] Pray (x) that our love grows into knowledge (y).

      [transition: What must our love produce?]

   B. [1:10a] Pray (x) that our love grows into discernment (y).

      [transition: What kind of discernment?]

      1. [1:10a] Pray (x) that our love grows into every kind of discernment (y).

         [transition: What kind of discernment?]

      2. [1:10a] Pray (x) that our love grows into the discernment of the more excellent things (y).

         [transition: What will discernment produce?]

      3. [1:10b] Discern the more excellent things (x) and you will be pure and blameless until the day of Christ (y).

         [transition: What is the purpose of our purity?]

II. [1:11] Our purity and blamelessness until the day of Christ (x) will glorify God (y).

   [transition: How can we be pure?]

   A. [1:11a] We will be pure and blameless (x) if we are filled with the fruit of righteousness that comes through Christ (y).

      [transition: What is the purpose of our purity?]

B. [1:11b] Our purity and blamelessness until the day of Christ (x) praises and glorifies God (y).[92]

Applying the Rhetorical Processes to the Homiletic Outline

As discussed *infra*, a proposition may be developed rhetorically in five ways: explanation (what does this proposition mean?), illustration (what does this proposition "look like"?), application (how should this proposition change our lives?), argumentation (why should we apply this proposition?), and exhortation (what encouragement is there to apply this proposition?). The homiletic outline consists of preachable, succinct, and salient propositions. The exegete may apply any one, any combination, or all the rhetorical processes to each proposition. The exegetical material derived by the study of the passage may spar the development of the rhetorical processes. The more exegetical content that is interwoven into the rhetorical development of each proposition, the more biblical the exegete's sermon will be. The more biblical the sermon is, the better it is. Great preaching is biblical preaching.

2.3 Observe the Key Words in the Sentences

What Are Words and Why Study Them?

Words are important because they are the means by which the Holy Spirit has chosen to speak. The Scripture is essentially a system of concepts. Words represent these concepts. Words symbolize the concepts God chose to inscripturate into His written Word. But the words of Scripture must not be construed as simplistic and stark. Words are microcosms. Each word may become an entire world of meaning. Furthermore, in one sense, the linguist may declare that "each word when used in a new context is a new word." Because words may have different meanings, but only one specific meaning in a specific context, each word must be studied for its general meaning and its meaning in a particular context. Although a word has many possible meanings, a word in context has only a

---

92. Ibid.

specific meaning in that context.[93] The exegete's goal is to know the literary, historical, cultural, linguistic, and situational context of any term's particular use. The intra and para biblical context is the key to a term's meaning. Truly, the exegete's cheer is "Context! Context! Context!"[94]

2.3a Determine which words require a full word study in light of the book's subject/complement, the paragraph subject/complement, the book's historical and cultural background, and theological controversy.

The Need to Prepare a Full Word Study

Time is a limited quantity for the exegete. A full word study may take more time than the exegete has. Dallas Seminary students, for instance, often take eight to fifteen hours to prepare a full word study. If a pastor spends thirty to thirty-five hours per week preparing sermons, a full word study may be impossible. It is necessary, nonetheless, for the exegete to acquire the skill of preparing a full word study for two reasons: (1) Preparing a full word study will open the exegete's horizons to how wide a field of meaning a particular word may have. An awareness of how wide a variety of nuances a word may have will give the exegete more insight into distinguishing between the possible meanings of a term and determining which meaning is appropriate in the context the exegete is studying. The discipline of preparing a full word study will give the exegete the "feel" of how to pick the semantic sense of a word. The semantic sense of a word is its precise meaning in a given context. (2) Further, the discipline of preparing a full word study will better acquaint the exegete with the strengths and weaknesses of the various concordances and lexicons. Using and comparing the various concordances and lexicons in the manner required for a full word study will develop for the exegete a "feel" for each tool. A seasoned exegete "feels at home" with the various linguistic tools.

---

93. See Grassmick's treatment of the Greek term for "word" (λογος) 144.

94. Unpublished class notes, Exegetical Method in Ephesians—203, Dallas Theological Seminary, Spring 1988.

The Book Subject/Complement as a Key to Choosing Which Words to Study

The overall subject/complement of a book of the Bible is a key to determine if a full word study should be undertaken. The book of Jonah is a striking example. Yahweh's speech to Jonah in the last paragraph of the last chapter encompasses the book's subject and complement. The book's subject is Yahweh's "compassion," the key term used in Yahweh's speech in the last paragraph of the last chapter. The book's complement is that this "compassion" extends beyond the visible church unto the unconverted. The term "compassion" is at the core of both the book's subject and complement. Not only is the term crucial to understanding the final divine speech of the book, it is crucial to understanding the book as a whole. Accordingly, a full word study of the term "compassion" would be wise for preaching and teaching the book of Jonah.

A Paragraph Subject/Complement as a Key to Choosing Which Words to Study

In some paragraphs of Scripture, a key word will appear numerous times. Often the repeated term is key to a paragraph's subject/complement. In the six verses of Romans 3:21–26, the term "righteousness" appears four times. The paragraph's subject is the righteousness of God. The paragraph's complement is that the righteousness of God is given by divine grace not by human works to those who believe. Because the term "righteousness" is central to the paragraph's subject/complement, preparing a full word study on the term would be wise.

A Book's Historical/Cultural Background as a Key to Choosing Which Words to Study

Some words in a passage of Scripture are strategic to understanding the passage because they introduce relevant background data. In Mark 7:9–13, for instance, Jesus rebuked the Pharisees for invalidating the Word of God by their own laws. The fifth commandment required that parents be honored, including by financial support. The Pharisees set aside the requirement of supporting parents financially by legislating the "corban" or gift (Mk. 7:11). If Israelites gave a "corban" to the temple, they were relieved by Pharisaic law of financially supporting their parents. A full word study on the Aramaic term "corban" would offer the exegete the necessary background data to illumine the passage.

Theological Controversy as a Key to Determine Which Words to Study

Some key words are subjects of theological controversy. Because these terms are subjects of disagreement, an exegete has the responsibility of clarifying debate and offering a biblical solution. The term "world," for instance, is a subject of debate in passages such as John 1:29 and 1 John 2:2. Universal redemptionists see the scope of the term as encompassing every man, woman, and child past, present, and future. Limited redemptionists see the scope of the term as encompassing every man, woman, and child past, present, and future who believe. The former see the term as all without exception; the latter see the term as all without distinction. A full word study on the term "world" would illumine which position is linguistically tenable. Further, analysis beyond the lexical level may be necessary to determine a verdict. In this case, lexical exegesis, as accomplished by a full word study, would reveal that both positions are linguistically tenable. Further analysis would be required therefore to settle the debate. Another term that is the subject of theological debate is the term "virgin" in Isaiah 7:14. Some interpret the Hebrew term as meaning "young woman" while others interpret the meaning of the term to be "virgin." A full word study would reveal that in every place this term appears in the Old Testament, the meaning derived from context is "virgin." Only later in Rabbinic literature did the term come to have a category of meaning of "young woman." The exegete is responsible to illumine for his hearers whatever passage he exegetes; moreover, the exegete is more responsible in some debated areas of Scripture to clarify and settle debate regarding meaning.

2.3b Procedure for a Full Hebrew or Aramaic Word Study

The goal of a full word study is to determine what were that author's thoughts that predicated the author's use of that term. As Margolis articulated the goal of verbal analysis, the exegete's goal is to:

> ... see with the author's eyes and rethink his thoughts, be he epic bard or dramatist or prophet or psalmist; but he can do more: he can bring to bear upon the single utterance or a piece of literature all the known facts backward and forward that stand in relation thereto.[95]

Reconstructing the author's thoughts about a term is a lengthy and painstaking process. As the usage of the term informed the author's use of the term, so the exegete, by acquainting himself with the usage of the term, must inform himself of the term's substance. If the term appears only once in Scripture, as over 1200 Hebrew terms appear in the OT, then usage can not be a key to a term's meaning, unless, of course, much contemporary extant literature in the same era is available. If no such comparison of contemporaneous usage is possible, as is almost always the case, then the term's etymology and cognate languages become the two chief avenues to determine the term's meaning.

Methodology for Etymological Study

Survey of a Word's Etymology

Survey by (1) scanning the introductory paragraphs in the major lexicons, HALOT, Koehler-Bumgardner, and Brown-Driver-Briggs for the word's root, its meaning, and the meaning of any derived stems, if any. Survey etymology also (2) by scanning the cognate languages to determine the historical development of the word, if any.

Interpretative Questions on Etymology

Using the introductory paragraphs of the major lexicons, ask the following interpretative questions relating to a word's etymology:

---

95. Max L. Margolis, "The Scope and Methodology of Biblical Philology," *JQR NS* 1 (1910, 1911):8–9.

(1) Do the cognate words listed in the lexicons have the same corresponding letters as the Hebrew or Aramaic root, or has a homonym been incorrectly listed? (2) Is there a common meaning to the root, derived stems, and cognate terms? If there is not a common meaning, is there any reasonable explanation for the changes in meaning? (3) Which pieces of lexical evidence are most relevant to the word in the era it appears in the context studied? (4) Do the Hebrew or Aramaic derived stems, even later Rabbinic ones, confirm a possible meaning for the term in the context studied?

Beware the Root Fallacy

Although etymology has its place in a full word study, the exegete must beware of the "root fallacy." Meaning of a word is derived from its usage rather than its etymology. Etymology has its place in consideration of meaning, especially as words change their meaning through the centuries. The ultimate court of appeal, however, of a word's meaning is its usage, not etymology. The classic development of this thesis is by James Barr. As Barr states, the "explanation of words is by their contexts." Roots are not the sum and substance of verbal analysis.[96] As Barr elaborates:

> The use of words is deeply influenced by past history; etymological studies may show how the word developed and shifted in its sense. However, the past history of usage is quite different from its ultimate etymological origin.[97]

With hapax legomenona (words which appear only one time) or words that appear only a few times, Barr articulates the importance of etymology:

> Etymology is particularly important for the identification and elucidation of rare words and hapax legomena. The Hebrew Bible has many such words, and these can often be elucidated only through comparison with words in Ugaritic, Akkadian, Arabic and other cognate

---

96. James Barr, *Comparative Philology and the Text of the Old Testament* (Oxford: Clarendon Press, 1968), 113.

97. Ibid., 108.

languages. But we shall see that the fact that a word may be identified as cognate in Arabic or Akkadian may not mean that it has the same meaning in Hebrew.[98]

The exegete should note root fallacy and its related error of faulty "etymologizing." The root fallacy is the faulty extrapolation that two words with the same root mean the same or similar concepts. Faulty "etymologizing" is giving excessive weight to the history of a word as against its usage in a particular era.[99]

Methodology for Study of a Word's Usage

Determine the Word's Categories of Meaning

The first step in studying a word's usage is to determine the word's categories of meaning. Words generally have more than one category of meaning. Survey the key Hebrew lexicons to determine the categories of meanings.[100]

Second, after making notations of the various categories of meanings assigned by the key lexicons, proceed through *Englishman's Hebrew Concordance* citation by citation, assigning each citation to a particular category. If time permits, the exegete should look up each passage to determine what that word means in that particular context. If the exegete then proceeds to a Hebrew lexicon, such as Mandelkern's, the exegete may notice different nuances for different stems. Further, the following citations should receive closer attention because they usually offer greater light into the word's meaning according to usage—citations by the same author, citations in the same era, and citations in the same kind of literature (narrative, poetic, prophetic, apocalyptic). If a term is usually used in the abstract, a literal use may especially illustrate its abstract meaning.

---

98. James Barr, *Semantics of Biblical Language* (Oxford: University Press, 1961), 158.

99. Unpublished class notes, "103—Introduction to Hebrew Exegesis," Dallas Theological Seminary, Fall, '87.

100. Ibid.

Third, pick a *locus classicus* or a key passage that illustrates that category of meaning. This *locus classicus* may be a milestone to mark the various usages in this category of meaning. Also, if the exegete can not fit a particular citation into one of the categories, simply assign it to more than one and make a notation of why that citation fits into more than category of meaning. By this phase of choosing a *locus classicus*, the exegete may differ from the opinions of the editors of the lexicons, and create new categories of meaning or merge categories cited by the lexicons.

Fourth, the exegete should compare synonyms and antonyms cited by the lexicons. The exegete may compare the differences of the term studied with the various synonyms and the differences between the synonyms. By such a comparison, the exegete may answer the interpretative question, "Why did the Holy Spirit use this exact nuance rather than other similar nuances offered by this word's synonyms?"

Compare Translations of the Word in the Context Studied, and If Necessary, in Other Contexts

If the exegete has the luxury of knowing Aramaic, Syriac, or Latin, or the time to translate the Aramaic, Syriac, and Latin translations, the light shed by the other translations could be helpful. The Greek translations, however, should provide the greatest source of illumination. When using a Greek translation, the exegete should be aware of the following concerns which should qualify the understanding of the word offered by the translation. (1) The exegete should be cognizant of the nature of the philosophy of the translation. The Septuagint, for instance, differs in translation philosophy from a quite literal to a more paraphrastic posture, depending on the book. (2) The exegete should be aware of the translation philosophy of the particular book. The Pentateuch, the Psalms, and the Minor Prophets tend to be more literal in the Septuagint. Job is so paraphrastic that it is of little use to the exegete. (3) Most importantly, the exegete should compare the passages in the Greek Testament where the Greek term appears. If the O.T. Greek translation is an accurate rendering of the Hebrew or Aramaic term, the exegete has the divinely inspired Greek Testament as a source of cross-references. The exegete, of course, must not presume that any Greek translation is always accurate. If however, a particular Septuagint translation is actually quoted in the N.T., the exegete may safely presuppose that Septuagint translation is accurate. The Greek N.T., because of its divine inspiration, could not include error, even if that error were the quotation of a widely accepted Greek translation. Where the Septuagint appears in the Greek N.T., in those segments the Septuagint is certainly an accurate translation. (4) Finally, compare the English translations, bearing in mind the translation philosophies and theological stance of the translators.

3. Validate Rival Interpretative Options

- 3.1 Isolate the nature of the validation—textual, lexical, syntactical, stylistic, historical, biblical theological, systematic theological, and/or contextual (how the passage relates to its context or Book as a whole).
- 3.2 List the interpretative options, including exegetical evidences for and against each option.
- 3.3 Prayerfully make an exegetical decision.
- 3.4 In light of the solved validation problem, formulate preaching points and apply the rhetorical processes.

Why Do Differing Interpretations Exist?

The Infinity of Scripture

One particular attribute of Scripture, often neglected in systematic theologies, is the infinity of Scripture. To illustrate, an interpreter could spend twenty years observing the whole of Scripture from a "bird's eye" view and not exhaust its contents. For instance, broad themes such as the Old Testament as preparation for Christ, the Gospels as an introduction to Christ, Acts as a proclamation of Christ, the Epistles as an interpretation of Christ, and Revelation as the consummation of Christ are each inexhaustible. Furthermore, thematic relations between particular books are inexhaustible, such as common elements in Genesis and Revelation, Joshua and Acts, and Proverbs and James. Further yet, Mark drew some of his knowledge of the ministry of Christ from Peter, and Paul from his companion Luke; there are, therefore, related elements in Mark and 1 and 2 Peter, and Luke-Acts and Pauline literature. Broad thematic relations are inexhaustible. But not only on the broad macroscopic view but also the detailed microscopic view is Scripture inexhaustible. To illustrate, an entire doctor of theology dissertation from Dallas Theological Seminary explores the phrase "in Christ" in Ephesians. The preposition "in" is examined alone, its use with "Christ," and the use of the phrase in each of its contexts in the Book of Ephesians. One could conceivably trace such a phrase through Old Testament themes of Yahweh being in and among his people, and the New Testament theme of an individual being indwelt by the Spirit. Furthermore, individual words such as truth, righteousness, salvation, hope, and holiness are inexhaustible. These terms are comprehensive terms which encompass a vast spectrum of doctrine. In sum, from whatever vantage point an interpreter approaches Scripture, "bird's eye" or "earthworm," Scripture is infinite because its Author is infinite.

Differing Interpretations

Interpretations differ for two reasons—the infinity of Scripture and the imperfections of the interpreter. Because Scripture is infinite, some material is direct and straightforward and other material is complex and profound. And, what is simple to one interpreter may be complex to another. Furthermore, there is no way that interpreters can rid themselves of the noetic effects of the Fall. Depravity extends to the mind. The sinful nature that resides in every interpreter will cause error if it can. As an interpreter comes to a more complex passage, he may surmise several possible meanings. The passage, however, may legitimately include more than one option. That is, the author's intended meaning might include more than one option. Conversely, the options that a particular interpreter surmises may all be wrong.

The result of differing interpretations is different denominations. As interpretations differ, those who hold to one interpretation will associate, being bound together by their common view or views. Denominations arise on major hermeneutic differences. Of course, minor hermeneutic differences arise in any denomination.

How Does an Interpreter Choose between Rival Interpretive Options?

The process by which an interpreter chooses between rival options is called validation.[101] The underlying principle of validation is in order for preaching to be effective, is must be authoritative; and in order for preaching to be authoritative, it must be true. Validation is the procedure to determine which interpretative option is true.

How to Arrive at a Final Decision

When the research is done, the exegete must make a final decision as to what option is right, or at least most probable. It is imperative that the exegete be aware of the most compelling reasons for and against the final verdict. This will help keep him from overbearing dogmatism on the one extreme and "wishy-washiness" on the other.[102] If the problem calls for a "close call" verdict—that is, an option that the exegete believes is just barely superior to another—the exegete should recheck the reasons for each view and determine which are primary and which are subsidiary. Further, it may be possible that the rivals are not really rivals at all but merely different aspects of an identical view. Most importantly, the exegete must be honest with his congregation, allowing them the

---

101. The following treatment of validation is largely an adaption of the method taught by the New Testament department of Dallas Theological Seminary. Furthermore, the author underscores there is perhaps no other single course known to him that will help a potential exegete more than "Exegetical Method in Ephesians." Therefore, the following is essentially a repackaging, summation, and slight modification.

102. Unpublished notes, "Validation," "204—Exegetical Method in Ephesians," Dallas Theological Seminary, Spring 1988.

courtesy of knowing that there are rival options which may have valid points undergirding them.[103]

FOURTH PHASE: ENLARGEMENT INTO DOCTRINE

4. Enlargement

- 4.1 Enlarge the text into doctrine, using the whole of Scripture.
- 4.2 Enlarge the text through verbal parallelism, conceptual parallelism, and typological parallelism.
- 4.3 Enlarge the text by consulting the standard biblical theologies, historic confessions, and systematic theologies.
- 4.4 Enlarge the text by consulting Puritan and Reformed commentaries.
- 4.5 Formulate preaching points and apply the rhetorical processes.

The Analogy of Faith or Analogy of Scripture Principle

The analogy of faith or analogy of Scripture interpretative principle derives from the unity principle of inspiration. As the one Author of creation formulated a harmonious and self-sustaining ecosystem on earth, so the one Author of Scripture codified a harmonious and self-completing Bible. Nature fits together; the Bible fits together. Unity pervades the diversity of nature; unity pervades the diversity of the Bible. Crampton, in his pamphlet *Biblical Hermeneutics*, cites 1 Corinthians 14:33, that the trumpet should not give an uncertain sound, in his defense of the harmony principle.[104] God's voice, often pictured in trumpet imagery (*cf.* Rev. 4:1ff.), never contradicts itself. Therefore, since the Author

---

103. Ibid.
104. Crampton, 10.

is not self-contradictory, what we understand Him to say in one place may illumine what we do not understand Him to say in another. The best interpreter of Scripture is Scripture.[105] The ultimate court of appeal in a controversy over what a text says is the rest of the Bible.

The Relation of Exegesis to the Analogy of Faith or Analogy of Scripture

Bernard Ramm is correct in his assertion that "exegesis is prior to any system of theology."[106] Before a theological system may be formulated, the exact nature of the pieces must be determined. Ramm elaborates: "The Scriptures are themselves the divine disclosure. From them is to be derived our system of theology. We can only know the truth of God by a correct exegesis of Scripture. Therefore exegesis is prior to any system of theology"[107] The historic Protestant position is to ground theology in Biblical exegesis. A theological system is to be built up exegetically brick by brick. Hence the theology is no better than the exegesis that underlies it. The task of the systematic theologian is to commence with these bricks ascertained through exegesis, and build the temple of his theological system.[108]

According to Romans 12:6, all who prophesy must do so according to the analogy of faith. The noun πιστις, or faith, has both active and passive senses in Scripture. The active sense, as in Romans 1:16–17 for instance, denotes the act of an individual believer exercising faith in the Lord; the passive sense, as in Jude

---

105. R.C. Sproul, *Knowing Scripture* (Downers Grove, Ill.: Intervarsity, 1978), 46.

106. For a brief but compelling discussion of the necessity for exegetical underpinnings for building systematic theology, see Bernard Ramm, *Protestant Biblical Interpretation* (Boston: Wilde, 1956), 1–7; unpublished notes, Biblical Theology handout, "204—Exegetical Method in Ephesians," Dallas Theological Seminary, Spring 1988.

107. Ramm, 1–7.

108. Ibid.

3–4, denotes the whole body of revealed truth from Genesis 1:1 to Revelation 22:21. The preposition ανα, usually translated "up," coupled with the noun λογια, or "words," means literally "words made upward." The apostle specifically commanded all who prophesy to do so according to the analogy of all of Scripture. Therefore, it is a necessary consequence that every exegete formulate the true analogy of Scripture. Correct systematic theology is commanded by the Apostle Paul (Rom. 12:6).

"Biblical Theology" an Intermediate Step between Exegesis and Systematic Theology

It is the biblically mandated goal of every exegete, therefore, to interpret the pieces, and correctly piece them together into a correct system of theology. An intermediate step between the exegete's interpretation of his text to enlargement into a theological system is Biblical theology. The exegete begins with one text. To formulate a theological system, he needs related texts. The process of determining what the relevant parallel passages are and what they contribute to the central text is the task of Biblical theology. The task of systematic theology is to organize the data and articulate the substance of the doctrines taught with accurate phraseology.

Biblical theology, therefore, is not an end in itself. It is a means to acquire clear and accurate systematic doctrine. C.C. Ryrie, in his introduction to his *Theology of the New Testament*, offers the following helpful definition of Biblical theology:

Biblical theology is that branch of theological science which deals systematically with the historically conditioned progress of the self-revelation of God as deposited in the Bible.[109]

---

109. C.C. Ryrie, *Biblical Theology of the New Testament* (Chicago: Moody, 1959), 17–19. Note that Ryrie does not hold that Biblical theology should replace systematic theology. He sees their role as complementary. Systematic theology is essential (1) for the refutation of heresy because heresies are systems of theology which contradict themselves and Scripture. Systematic theology is also essential (2) for the orderly teaching of the doctrines of Scripture. Further, systematic theology is also necessary (3) for balanced application of Scripture. The last section of this thesis, "Casuistry or the Uses of the Text," will

The key phrase is the "historically conditioned progress." Biblical theological discipline traces components of theology through the various epochs of revelation. These components are analyzed first in their native context and historical and cultural environment, then for their contribution to systematic theology as a whole. Further, Ryrie reiterates:

Biblical Theology ... systematizes the truth as it was progressively revealed through the various writers.[110]

Thus, Biblical theology is concerned with when and to whom the truth was given; systematic theology is concerned with what truth was given and how it interrelates with the whole of Scripture. Further, Ryrie says:

Biblical Theology goes beyond exegesis, for it not only presents what the writer said but seeks to discover the theological pattern in his mind, of which the writing was a reflection.

Concerning the matter of theological patterns, George Eldon Ladd in his *Theology of the New Testament*, elaborates:

Biblical Theology has the task of expounding the theology found in the Bible in its own historical setting, and its own terms, categories, and thought forms.[111]

Thus, through Biblical theology the exegete seeks to enlarge his text in light of other passages, in their own historical setting, in their own terms, categories, and thought forms. By allowing parallel passages to speak in the historical and cultural milieu of their authors, and reconstructing the authors' theological system and worldview,[112] the data gathered may enlarge the exegete's text, adding substance, clarification, and power.

---

discuss the use of systematic theology in application.

110. Ryrie, 21; Ryrie's thirteen pages, 11–24, on the nature, method, and function of Biblical theology is an excellent introduction to this discipline.

111. George Eldon Ladd, *A Theology of the New Testament* (Grand Rapids: Eerdmans, 1974).

112. Unpublished notes, Biblical Theology handout, 204—Exegetical Method in Ephesians, Dallas Theological Seminary, Spring 1988.

The Method of Biblical Theological Research

The method of Biblical theological research has three foci—cultural milieu, historical milieu, and authorial usage. Note, however, that the concerns of cultural and historical milieu for the exegete's text itself should have been considered prior to the exegetical process on the central text, as described in 2:1ff. The concerns of Biblical theology for cultural and historical milieu relate to the parallel passages which relate to the central text under consideration. Cultural milieu consists in those forces which affect the author from the standpoint of his personal heritage—occupation, living conditions, cultural influences. The author cues us to these influences through his references and allusions to people, institutions, and practices.[113] Paul's background of Rabbinic training under Gemaliel and being a Pharisee would be valuable in interpreting a variety of his statements, such as "we are the circumcision" in Philippians 3:3 and Colossians 2:9–11. Historical milieu refers to the historical background and hence the influences upon the author's thinking and scope of concern. Paul's witnessing the use of heavy infantry during the revolt of Cilicia in his childhood casts light on his reference to the spiritual armor in Ephesians 6:10–20.

Another focus of Biblical theology is authorial usage. Authorial usage refers to "the way the author uses specific words and develops themes built upon and around those words."[114] If the exegete has performed a full word study upon key terms according to 2.3, research from parallel passages can help enlarge his text. Further, the exegete can use Moulton and Geden's *Greek Concordance* to trace the use of key phrases. At the top of each word list in Moulton and Geden are key associated words or phrases, which may be traced by simply scanning the word list. Some articles in Bauer, Arndt, and Gingrich's *Greek Lexicon* treat recurring phrases that a particular author uses. Also, Kittel's *Theological Dictionary of the New Testament* and the *New International Dictionary of New Testament Theology* have lengthy articles that deal with authorial

---

113. Ibid.
114. Ibid.

usage of phrases.[115] Further, there is a marginally helpful English work that solely traces phrases in the King James Version and Revised Standard Version, the *Phrase Concordance of the Bible*.[116] The latter work may be helpful as an introductory tool to explore authorial usage of phrases.

Fourth Phase: Enlargement into Doctrine

4. Enlargement

   4.1 Enlarge the text into doctrine, using the whole of Scripture.

   4.2 Enlarge the text through verbal parallelism, conceptual parallelism, and typological/anti-typological parallelism.

   4.3 Enlarge the text by consulting the standard biblical theologies, historic confessions, and systematic theologies.

   4.4 Enlarge the text by consulting Puritan and Reformed commentaries.

   4.5 Formulate preaching points and apply the rhetorical processes.

ENLARGEMENT THROUGH VERBAL PARALLELISM

The verbal parallelism described is not to be confused with the full word-study procedure outlined in 2.3d. The enlargement process in this section is actually an extension of a full word study. In enlargement, the exegete seeks those passages that included not only the key word or words in his text, but also important theological contribution to meaning of that word. For instance, if the exegete's text were Romans 1:16–17, "for therein is the righteousness of God revealed," the exegete probably would need a full word study on the

---

115. Ibid.

116. *Phrase Concordance of the Bible*. (Nashville: Nelson, 1984).

word "righteousness." In the process of comparing other passages with the word "righteousness," certain passages make especially important contributions, such as Romans 3:21-22. This passage would clarify that the righteousness of which Paul speaks is "apart from the law" and comes "from God through faith in Jesus Christ." Romans 5:19 would add the important facts that "righteousness" is part of "God's abundant provision of grace" and "gift." Further, Romans 6:20 adds that the believer should yield his life in "slavery to righteousness leading to holiness." Enlargement, therefore, allows important theological facts from other theology-laden passages to usher in understanding to the exegete's texts.

ENLARGEMENT THROUGH CONCEPTUAL PARALLELISM

In a manner similar to enlargement through verbal parallelism, the exegete may enlarge his text through conceptual parallelism. Unlike verbal parallelism, there is no definite clue to find other passages whose theology will illumine the exegete's text. To find other passages that will illumine a text, the exegete may be forced to rely upon his own knowledge of the English Bible. The need to know "off the cuff" parallel texts underscores the need for regular systematic Bible reading. There is no substitute for general Bible knowledge. There are, however, other ways for the exegete to find other passages that conceptually parallel his text. One particular work designed to offer conceptually parallel passages is *The Treasury of Scripture Knowledge*.[117] Other sources of theologically relevant parallel passages are commentaries. By seeking helpful parallels in other parts of Scripture, the exegete can present to his hearers a "mini-theological system" of passages that illumine his central text. Another newer work which is the first of its kind is Elwell's *Topical Analysis of the Bible*.[118] The work organizes Scripture

---

117. Caine, Browne, Blayney, Scott, et. al., *The Treasury of Scripture Knowledge* (Old Tappan, N.J.: Revell, n. d.)

118. Walter A. Elwell, ed. *Topical Analysis of the Bible* (Grand Rapids: baker, 1991).

by topic. The heads of its sections are either words or phrases or Biblical concepts. Although all of the various topical Bibles, among them *Nave's* and *Zondervan's*, are useful tools in this area, Elwell's work is unique in aiding in the enlargement of a text.

One method of enlargement of an entire book of the Bible is to list all the propositions in the books, then systematize them logically. The propositions may be ordered by the most overarching down to the smallest detail. They may be categorized and subcategorized. God's perfection in all of His thoughts necessitates that He be logical in all of His thoughts. Therefore, when God speaks to us in an entire book of the Bible, the concepts contained in the book must have some logical interrelation. Although the chronological order of these concepts may not appear logical to us, all of the major concepts in a book of the Bible can be rearranged into a logically impeccable order. The following is a sample introduction to a systematic enlargement of Malachi.

The Book of Malachi, for instance, bears the overarching message that God condemns spiritual hypocrisy. All of the concepts in the book may be classified under three logically interrelated heads. First, why does God condemn hypocrisy? The passages that explain His holy character and His work for His people fall under this head. Secondly, the book describes how God condemns spiritual hypocrisy. Passages that demonstrate spiritual hypocrisy include the dialogues, direct condemnations, and illustrations of the people's hypocrisy. Thirdly, the book describes the result of God's condemnation; this result is twofold. Negatively, the people may continue in their hypocrisy and receive judgment. Positively, they may repent and enjoy God's covenant blessings. The following outline is an example of doctrinal enlargement of the book of Malachi.

The "card-stacking" method of ordering the propositions logically can be extremely effective in introducing a congregation to an entire book of the Bible. By seeing the theology of the entire book organized into a coherent, logically organized whole, they may more readily receive the theological message intended for them.

ENLARGEMENT THROUGH TYPOLOGY

Type (τυπος), antitype (αντιτυπος), shadow (σκια), and allegory (αλλεγορια)[119] are each key New Testament terms that describe recurring patterns of thought in Scripture. Types are Old Testament patterns that find their fulfillment in New Testament counterparts. The Passover, for instance, finds its New Testament fulfillment in the Lord's Supper. The Passover is the type; the Lord's Supper the antitype. If the exegete's text included the Passover, parallel thought from Lord's Supper texts would be helpful to understand present-day application. Conversely, if the exegete's text included the Lord's Supper, parallel thought from Old Testament Passover texts would be helpful to understand the nature of the Lord's Supper.

The two helpful reference tools in typology are Benjamen Keach's *Preaching and Teaching from the Types and Metaphors of the Bible* and Patrick Fairbairn's *Typology of Scripture*. The exegete should check the index of this work for his text and the table of contents for other types or metaphors which may parallel his text's subject/complement.

4.3 Enlarge the Text by Consulting the Standard Biblical Theologies, Historic Confessions, and Systematic Theologies

THE USE OF THE STANDARD BIBLICAL THEOLOGIES

A variety of Biblical theologies are outstanding in the field and constitute a "must" for the exegete. The exegete may use the Biblical theologies in either of two ways. First, he may simply check the index in the back of each for his text and consult the appropriate pages. Or, he may scan the table of contents for that section of the work that parallels the subject/complement of his text.

---

119. "Type, anti-type, shadow, and allegory."

HOW TO COMMUNICATE BIBLICAL CONTENT

The Key Biblical Theologies include:

Old Testament Biblical Theologies

Dempster, Stephen. *Dominion and Dynasty: A Biblical Theology of the Hebrew Bible.*

Oehler, Gustav. *The Theology of the Old Testament.*

Payne, J. Barton. *A Theology of the Older Testament.*

Zuck, Roy. *A Biblical Theology of the Old Testament.*

New Testament Biblical Theologies

Beale, G.K. *New Testament Biblical Theology.*

Ladd, George. *A Theology of the New Testament.*

Lehman, Chester. *A Theology of the New Testament.*

Ryrie, Charles. *A Biblical Theology of the New Testament.*

Zuck, Roy. *A Biblical Theology of the New Testament.*

Biblical Theologies of the Entire Bible

Alexander, T. Desmond. *From Eden to the New Jerusalem.*

Gentry, Peter. *Kingdom through Covenant: A Biblical-Theological Understanding of the Covenants*

Goldsworthy, Graeme. *Christ-Centered Biblical Theology.*

Hafeman, Scott. *Central Themes in Biblical Theology.*

Hamilton, James. *What is Biblical Theology?*

Owen, John. *Biblical Theology.*

Vos, Gerhardus. *The Theology of the Old Testament.*

THE USE OF THE HISTORIC CONFESSIONS

In a similar fashion, the exegete may use historic confessions. First, he may check indexes for his particular text. Or, he may scan the heads of the confessions for the particular heads that parallel the subject/complement of his text. Key confessions include

- The Westminster Confession of Faith (1646) with Larger and Shorter Catechisms (1648)
- Apostles Creed (2nd century)
- The Heidelberg Catechism (1563 catechism of the Dutch Reformation)
- The Canons of the Synod of Dordt (1618–19; articulates the biblical paramaters of anthropology, soteriology, and decrees of God)
- The Belgic Confession (1561; revised 1619)
- The First Helvitic Confession (A.D. 1536; Swiss reformers Bullinger and Bucer's work)
- Geneva Confession (A.D. 1536; Swiss reformers Calvin and Farel's work)
- The Second Helvetic Confession
- Scots Reformed Confession (A.D. 1560; John Knox's work)
- Cambridge Platform (1648) and The Savoy Declaration (1658)
- Gallic Confession
- The London Confession of Faith (1677)
- The Philadelphia Confession of Faith (1742)
- Nicene Creed (developed from Council of Nicea and Council of Constantinople A.D. 381; articulates the biblical parameters of the deity and humanity of Christ)
- Athanasian Creed (articulates the biblical parameters of the doctrine of the Trinity)

The Chicago Statement on Inerrancy (this work is currently a standard articulation of the doctrines of the inspiration, infallibility, and inerrancy of Scripture)

The Use of the Standard Systematic Theologies

If Biblical theology seeks to determine the thinking of a biblical author on a particular topic, systematic theology seeks to determine what the thinking of the whole of Scripture is on a particular topic. Systematic theology is an expansion of Biblical theology in that it seeks to weave together the thinking of all the Biblical authors into a cohesive whole.

The formulation of and regular use of systematic theology is imperative because heresies are, in effect, erroneous systematic theologies. Arianism is an erroneous systematic theology of the Trinity; the "Jesus only" cult represents an erroneous systematic theology of the Trinity; antinomianism is an erroneous systematic theology of the law of God; and the works salvation doctrine is an erroneous systematic theology of salvation. In sum, systematic theology without error must be formulated from Scripture, and correct systematic theology will help keep the exegete from the heresies of his day. Some of the recommended systematic theologies have been out of print for more than a century. Currently however, the Banner of Truth Trust[120] is reprinting some Puritan works. Further, the exegete may seek the used book lists of David Lachman and Curt Daniel.[121] Key systematic theologies include:

Baxter, Richard. *Catholick Theologie*. This work, though the most prolific of the Puritan authors, is designed to focus on the common ground to which all Reformation Protestants held, including Melancthonian and more moderate Lutherans.[122]

---

120. Current catalogs may be obtained from The Banner of Truth Trust, P.O. Box 621, Carlisle, PA 17015.

121. David Lachman and Curt Daniel are well known in Reformed circles as used Reformed booksellers. Both Lachman and Daniel are skilled at finding out of print Puritan theologies and commentaries.

122. London: Robert White, 1675, reprint edition by Curt Daniel.

Berkhof, Louis. *Systematic Theology*. Extremely valuable because of its clarity and brevity.

Breckinridge, Robert J. *The Knowledge of God, Objectively Considered* and *The Knowledge of God, Subjectively Considered*. This complete Reformed theology is somewhat a moderating vantage point from the Princetonian Calvinism of Hodge, Alexander, and Warfield to the north and the Southern Calvinism of Thornwell and Dabney.[123]

Boyce, James P. *An Abstract of Systematic Theology*. Boyce's work provides a brief but thorough treatment of the standard theological heads.

Calvin, John. *Institutes of the Christian Religion*. Perhaps the greatest systematic theology ever written.

Hill, George. *Lectures in Divinity*. These lectures, along with the works of Thomas Boston and Thomas Chalmers, provide the cream of Scottish Calvinism.

Hodge, Charles. *Systematic Theology*. A standard.

Morris, Edward D. *Theology of the Westminster Symbols*. This commentary on the Westminster Confession is twice the length of that of A.A. Hodge.[124]

Pictet, Benedict. *Christian Theology*. Pictet and Turretin together represent the cream of the Swiss Reformation.[125]

Ridgely, Thomas. *A Body of Divinity*. This is a complete Reformed theology built around the Larger Catechism; it is however more moderate than other Reformed theologies.[126]

Shedd, G.T. *Dogmatic Theology*. Another excellent standard theology.

Smith, Morton. *Notes on Systematic Theology*. For years Smith's notes from Reformed Seminary and now Greenville

---

123. New York: Robert Carter, 1858–59, reprint edition by Curt Daniel.

124. Columbus: The Champion Press, 1900, reprint edition by Curt Daniel.

125. London: R.B. Seeley and W. Burnside, 1834, reprint edition by Curt Daniel.

126. Ridgely, Thomas. *A Body of Divinity*. New York: Robert Carter, 1855, reprint edition by Curt Daniel.

Presbyterian Theological Seminary have provided the theological foundation of many Reformed ministers.

Usher, James. *A Body of Divinitie*. This tome is an important work by an Anglican Calvinist. Its chief strength is its question and answer format.[127]

Wardlaw, Ralph. *Systematic Theology*.[128] This work is one of the largest Reformed systematic theologies ever written. Most subjects are treated in great detail.

4.4 Enlarge the Text by Consulting Puritan and Reformed Commentaries

The Use of Puritan Commentaries

Because Puritan commentaries follow the basic form of Puritan sermons—exposition, doctrine, and application—the doctrinal enlargements in the Puritan works serve as models for enlargements by the modern exegete. Not only will the exegete gain preaching material *per se* from the Puritan expositions, including a wealth of illustrations, but also gain a knack for enlargement that can come only by observing the masters.

A listing of the Puritan commentaries on each book of the Bible is available from Spurgeon's *Commenting and Commentators*.[129] Since there is perhaps no better list available, the exegete should consult that list, searching for commentaries written in the Puritan era, approximately 1540 to 1700. Spurgeon's *Commenting and Commentators* should be the buying guide for Puritan works.

---

127. London: T. Downes and George Badger, 1653, reprint edition by Curt Daniel.

128. Edinburgh, Adam and Charles Black, 1856, reprint edition by Curt Daniel.

129. Charles Haddon Spurgeon, *Commenting and Commentaries* (Grand Rapids: Kregel, 1954).

AN ABBREVIATED LIST OF RECOMMENDED PURITAN COMMENTARIES

The Bible as a Whole

  Assembly of Divines, at Westminster

  John Diodati

  Dutch Annotations, by the Synod of Dort

  Joseph Hall

  Matthew Henry

  Edward Leigh (from Job to the Song of Songs and the entire NT)

  John Mayer

  Christopher Ness

  Matthew Poole

  John Trapp

  William Wall

  Thomas Wilson

  Old Testament

  Arthur Jackson

  John Richardson

Pentateuch

  Henry Ainsworth

  Gervase Babington

  Richard Kidder

  James Aurin

  Abarham Wright

Genesis

  George Hughes

Josias Shute

Andrew Willet

Exodus

Andrew Willet

The Decalogue

Lancelot Andrews

Peter Barker

John Dod and Robert Cleaver

James Durham

Edward Fisher

Ezekial Hopkins

John Weemse

William Whateley

Leviticus

Samuel Mather

Benjamen Keach

John Weemse

Andrew Willet

Numbers

William Attersoll

Deuteronomy

John Calvin's sermons[130]

A Harmony of the Pentateuch

---

130. John Calvin is listed in this Puritan list because of his mentorship and influence upon the early Puritans.

John Calvin

Joshua
> John Calvin

Judges
> Richard Rogers
> Francis Quarles

Ruth
> Richard Bernard
> Thomas Fuller
> Lewis Lavater
> Edward Topsell

1 and 2 Samuel
> Andrew Willet
> William Guild
> Samuel, Saul, and David
> Patrick Delaney
> John Marbeck
> Solomon's Temple
> John Bunyan
> Samuel Lee
> Elijah and Elisha
> Daniel Rogers

Esther
> Thomas Cooper

Edward Leigh

Thomas Wilcox

Job

  George Abbot

  Theodore Beza

  R. Blackmore

  John Calvin's sermons

  Joseph Caryl

  James Durham

  George Hutchinson

  Francis Quarles

  J.F. Senault

Psalms

  George Abbot

  Victor Bythner

  John Calvin

  David Dickson

  Henry Hammond

  William Nicholson

  Charles Haddon Spurgeon

  Thomas Wilcox

  Samuel Woodford

  Abraham Wright

  Portions of the Book of Psalms

  Richard Baker

  John Boys

Robert Rollock

Vistorinus Strigellius

Penitential Psalms

Richard Baker

John Donne

John Fisher

John Hayward

Archibald Simpson

Separate Psalms
- Samuel Smith, Ps. 1
- Matthew Stonham, Ps. 1
- Thomas Horton, Ps. 2, 42, 51, 63
- Christopher Cartwright, Ps. 15
- George Dawname, Ps. 15
- Richard Turnball, Ps. 15
- Nicholas, Bownd, Ps. 20:1–6
- Richard Baker, Ps. 23
- John Hooper, Ps. 23, 62, 73, 77

Obadiah Sedgwick, on the "Shepherd of Israel"
- Samuel Smith, Ps. 23
- Robert Mossom, Ps. 25
- Thomas Pierson, Ps. 27, 84, 85, 87
- Robert Leighton, Ps. 32
- Thomas Taylor, Ps. 32
- Richard Sibbes, Ps. 42, 130
- W. Troughton, Ps. 45

Samuel Hieron, Ps. 51

Arthur Hildersham, Ps. 51

Samuel Page, Ps. 51

Samuel Smith, Ps. 51, 90

Edward Parry, Ps. 73

Thomas Hall, Ps. 82

Nicholas Heminge, Ps. 84

Gerard Hyperius, Ps. 107

Edward Reynolds, Ps. 110

William Gouge, Ps. 116

William Cowper, Ps. 119

Richard Greenham, Ps. 119

Thomas Manton, Ps. 119

George Hutchinson, Ps. 130

Robert Leighton, Ps. 130

John Owen, Ps. 130

Proverbs
- Robert Allen
- John Dod
- Michael Jermin
- Peter Muffet
- Thomas Wilcocks

Ecclesiastes
- Annotations edited by J. Streater
- Theodore Beza
- Hugh Broughton

John Cotton
Thomas Granger
Michael Jermin
Alexander Nisbet
William Pemble
John Serranus or De Serres
F. Ycard
John Smith

Song of Songs
   Henry Ainsworth
   John Baptist Elias Avrillon
   Theodore Beza
   T. Beverly
   Thomas Brightman
   John Collinges
   John Cotton
   John Dove
   James Durham
   Robert Fleming
   William Guild
   George Gyffard
   Nathaniel Homes
   John Robotham
   Richard Sibbes
   Thomas Wilcocks
   Samuel Woodward (paraphrase)

Prophets
  William Lowth

Isaiah
  John Calvin
  Parts of Isaiah
  James Durham, Is. 53
  Thomas Manton, Is. 53

Jeremiah and Lamentations
  John Hull
  Daniel Swift
  John Udall

Ezekiel
  William Alliene (last nine chapters)
  William Greenhill (lengthiest commentary on Ezekiel ever written)

Daniel
  Thomas Brightman
  Hugh Broughton
  Ephraim Huit
  Henry More
  Thomas Parker
  Andrew Willet
  Minor Prophets
  Lambert Danaeus or Daneau
  George Hutchinson

Hosea
- Jeremiah Burroughes
- John Downame (chapters one through four)
- Edward Pocock
- Samuel Smith (chapter six)
- Edward Reynolds (chapter fourteen)
- Richard Sibbes (chapter fourteen)

Joel
- Samuel Chandler
- Edward Pocock
- Edward Topsell
- John Udall

Amos
- Sebastian Benefield
- Thomas Hall

Obadiah
- Edward Marbury
- James Pilington
- John Reynolds

Jonah
- George Abbott
- John Calvin
- Thomas Fuller
- John Hooper
- John King

Francis Quarles

Micah
  Edward Pocock
  Habbakuk
  Edward Marbury

Haggai
  John James Grynaeus
  John Rainolds

Zechariah

  William Pemble

Malachi
  Edward Pocock
  Richard Stock
  Thomas Watson

New Testament
  Richard Baxter
  John Boys
  William Burkitt
  Robert Gell
  Norton Knatchbull
  Edward Leigh
  John Mayer
  Pasquier Quesnell
  William Wall

Daniel Whitby

Four Gospels
  Samuel Clarke
  Harmonies of the Gospels
  John Calvin
  John Lightfoot

Matthew
  Isaac De Beausobre and Jaques L'Enfant
  Christopher Blackwood
  David Dickson
  Augustine Marloratus
  David Ward

Mark
  George Petter

John
  George Hutchinson
  Arthur Hildersham
  Anthony Burgess
  George Newton

Acts
  George Benson
  John Calvin
  Rodulphus Gualtherus
  John Lightfoot

Thomas Cartwright
Various Epistles
George Benson
David Dickson
James Ferguson
John Locke

Romans
   John Calvin
   Peter Martyr
   Andrew Willt
   Thomas Wilson
   W. Sclater
   Edward Elton
   Hugh Binnig
   Thomas Horton

1 and 2 Corinthians
   John Calvin
   John Colet

Galatians
   John Calvin
   Thomas Lushington
   William Perkins

Ephesians
   Paul Bayne
   John Calvin

Lancelot Ridley

Philippians
  Henry Airay
  John Calvin
  Jean Daille
  Colossians
  Paul Bayne
  Nicholas Byfield
  John Calvin
  Thomas Cartwright
  Nicholas Lockyer

1 and 2 Thessalonians
  John Jewel
  William Sclater
  W. Bradshaw
  Thomas Manton
  John Squire
  Pastoral Epistles
  John Calvin

1 and 2 Timothy
  John Barlow
  Thomas Hall
  Thomas Taylor

Philemon
  William Attersoll

Daniel Dyke
William Jones

Hebrews
  David Dickson
  Robert Duncan
  William Gouge
  G. Lawson
  John Owen

Parts of Hebrews
  Edward Deering
  Thomas Manton
  William Perkins

James
  John Adam
  Bernard Jacobi
  Thomas Manton
  John Mayer
  Richard Turnball

1 and 2 Peter
  William Ames

1 Peter
  William Alley
  Nicholas Byfield
  Robert Leighton

John Rogers

2 Peter
> Thomas Adams
> Archibald Symson

1 John
> Hugh Binnig
> John Calvin
> John Cotton
> Nathaniel Hardy

Jude
> William Jenkyn
> Thomas Manton
> Samuel Otes
> William Perkins
> Andrew Willet

Revelation
> Thomas Brightman
> William Cowper
> Samuel Chadock
> Charles Daubuz
> James Durham

This list is by no means exhaustive and does not intend to discount other excellent Reformation works, such as Luther's or Melancthon's. But the Puritan era, unlike any era since the time of the Apostles, produced balanced works which were exegetical but not spiritually dry, systematic but not impractical, devotional but not without Biblical substance.

There are three ways the exegete can access these Puritan writings. First, because most of these works are still out of print, the exegete's best hope is in Banner of Truth, Sprinkle, and Stillwaters Revival reprints, used book merchants such as Lachman and Daniel, and well-stocked theological libraries. Second, the exegete can seek out the indexes of major Puritan sets, of, for instance Owen, Charnock, Sibbes, Baxter, Manton, Swinnock, Goodwin, Brooks, and Boston. Through the indexes the exegete can find either the text under consideration or a related text, or the exegete can look under the topical heads. By such indexing the exegete can access Puritan comment. Third, the exegete can access Puritan comment through Spurgeon's volumes. Spurgeon had perhaps the finest Puritan library in all of Europe and consulted the Puritan works to prepare his sermons. Spurgeon's *Expository Encyclopedia* and the *Metropolitan Tabernacle Pulpit* are thoroughly indexed according to texts and topics.

A Systematization of a Book through the Card-Stacking Method

God's perfection in all of His thoughts necessitates that He be logical in all of His thoughts. Therefore, when God speaks to us in an entire book of the Bible, the concepts contained in the book must have some logical interrelation. Although the chronological order of these concepts may not appear logical to us, all of the major concepts in a book of the Bible can be rearranged into a logically impeccable order. The following is a sample introduction to a systematic enlargement of Malachi.

The Book of Malachi, for instance, bears the overarching message that God condemns spiritual hypocrisy. All of the concepts in the book may be classified under three logically interrelated heads. First, why does God condemn hypocrisy? The passages that explain His holy character and His work for His people fall under this head. Secondly, the book describes how God condemns spiritual hypocrisy. Passages that demonstrate spiritual hypocrisy include the dialogues, direct condemnations, and illustrations of the people's hypocrisy. Thirdly, the book describes the result of God's condemnation; this result is twofold. Negatively, the people may continue in their hypocrisy and receive judgment. Positively, they may repent and enjoy God's covenant blessings.

The "card-stacking" method can be extremely effective in introducing a congregation to an entire book of the Bible. By seeing the theology of the entire book organized into a coherent, logically organized whole, they may more readily receive the theological message intended for them.

FIFTH PHASE

Casuistry or the Uses of the Text

5. Application/Casuistry

   5.1 Perform a casuistic treatment upon the text to determine its uses.

   5.2 Prepare one's heart through prayer, particularly (1) by determining personally to obey the text regardless of loss of convenience, prestige, or position, (2) by asking the Lord for wisdom not to apply the text beyond its limits or to strip the text's content, and (3) by asking the Lord for God-given care for those to whom the text applies.

   5.3 Brainstorm: List every conceivable scenario to which the text may apply. The "cases" to which the text may apply is casuistry. Then list corresponding questions about how the text would change each scenario. The changes to each case are the "uses" of the text.

   5.4 Verify that each change would not violate the analogy of Scripture.

   5.5 Compare one's own "uses" with the "uses" in the Puritan commentaries. Add to or refine one's list accordingly.

   5.6 Each "use" is a preaching point. Develop each preaching point through the rhetorical processes.

WHAT IS CASUISTRY?

The term "casuistry" was common among the Puritans. It simply means applying Scripture to particular cases. During the counter-reformation another organization founded by Ignatius Loyola, the Jesuits, developed its own form of casuistry. Because the Jesuitical casuistry included how to strain the truth (i.e., how and when it is "right" to lie), the term fell out of repute among Protestants. It is quite ethical that such unbiblical forms of casuistry be dismissed, but the science and art of applying exegesis to particular cases of life is still imperative. The science of casuistry should be revived in the Church. It is a scientific and artful means of determining courses of behavior in particular circumstances.

Law students engage in casuistry. In the typical Socratic law class, a legal principle is posited, and students must apply the legal principle to every conceivable scenario. They must ask, exhaustively, "what if?" Every law school has compulsive "what if'ers"—those students who can not stop asking "what if?"

CASUISTRY/APPLICATION BIBLICALLY MANDATED

Casuistry, or application of Scripture, is a matter, at least in theory, that all professing Christians agree is a necessity. How application is to be performed, however, is subject to a wide diversity of opinion. A. W. Pink agrees:

> All professing Christians are agreed, in theory at least, that it is the bounden duty of those who bear His name to honour and glorify Christ in this world. But as to how this is to be done, as to what he requires from us to this end, there is wide difference of opinion. Many suppose that honouring Christ simply means to join some "church," take part in and support its various activities. Others think that honouring Christ signifies little more than making liberal financial contributions to His cause. Few indeed realize that Christ is honoured only as we

live holily unto him, and that, by walking in subjection to His revealed will.[1]

Approximately 2000 years before Pink, the prophet Samuel articulated a similar point: "Behold, to obey is better than sacrifice, and to hearken than the fat of rams" (1 Sam. 15:22). Later prophets echoed the same theme: "What doth the Lord require of thee, but to do justly, and to love mercy, and to walk humbly with thy God?" (Micah 6:8). "Let us hear the conclusion of the whole matter: Fear God, and keep his commandments: for this is the whole duty of man" (Eccl. 12:13). Additionally, the New Testament echoes the same motif: "And why call ye me, Lord, Lord, and do not the things which I say?" (Luke 6:46). "And that servant, which knew his lord's will, and prepared not himself, neither did according to his will, shall be beaten with many stripes" (Luke 12:47). True faith, according to Paul, is "the acknowledging of the truth which is after godliness" (Titus 1:1). "Be ye doers of the word, and not hearers only, deceiving your own selves" (James 1:22). "He that saith, I know him, and keepeth not his commandments, is a liar, and the truth is not in him" (1 John 2:4).[2]

THE ROLE OF THE HOLY SPIRIT IN CASUISTRY

The Spirit is the Applicator. This is not in the sense of *revelatio continua*, or continuing special revelation, but continuing illumination (cf. Phil. 3:15), understanding granted by the Spirit how a text changes any scenario, including the scenario of one's own character.[3] Only a right relationship to the Spirit is a fructifying relationship.[4] The interpreter is a fellow worker (συνεργος; 1 Cor. 3:9) with the Spirit. This means the effort to apply is not fifty percent divine and fifty percent human, but one hundred percent

---

1. A.W. Pink, *Profiting from the Word* (London: Banner of Truth, 1970), 69.
2. Ibid., 70–71.
3. Jon Veenhof, "The Holy Spirit and Holy Scripture," *The Interpretation of Scripture Today* (submitted to the RES Theological Conference, Chicago 1984).
4. Ibid., 13.

divine and one hundred percent human.⁵ Application is fully an act of God's Spirit, and fully an act of God's servants. In the interpretation process, the Spirit and the interpreter are a "communing council";⁶ similarly, in the application process, the interpreter and the Spirit, according to Veenhof, become a unit whereby the Spirit illumines, witnesses, comforts, and admonishes the interpreter. Guided by the Spirit, the interpreter personally not only knows but experiences Scripture, so that he can say authoritatively, "thus saith the Lord."⁷

THE GOAL OF CASUISTRY

The goal of casuistry is transformation by the Spirit—not transformation of self by self, but transformation of self by the external, divine force of the Spirit.⁸ This self-transformation is described verbally in Romans 12:2 and pictorially in 2 Corinthians 3:3. In Romans 12:2, a pregnant term, transliterated "metamorphosis," means a change of form, particularly a change of character.

THE FUNCTION OF CASUISTRY

Luther and Calvin maintained that the Christian is not only "free from the law" but also "free unto the law." Although justification frees the Christian from the law's condemnation (Rom. 6:14), in sanctification, the Spirit enables the Christian to live according to the righteousness of the law (Rom. 8:1–4).⁹ Casuistry is the process of conforming to God's written standards.

---

5. Ibid., 9–10.
6. Ibid., 14.
7. Ibid.
8. Compare the statements of Jack Kuhatschek, *Taking the Guesswork Out of Applying the Bible* (Downers Grove, Ill.: Intervarsity, 1990), 24. "As we immerse ourselves in Scripture, our goal is to develop within ourselves the mind and heart of God. We want to be able to think and to respond to every situation the way God himself would."
9. Gordon Spykman, "How Is the Scripture Normative in Christian

FIFTH PHASE

TESTS OF CASUISTRY

There are several earmarks of the casuistical process. Each one of these will be present, to varying degrees of course, if profitable application occurs.

One is properly performing a casuistical treatment when, first, one discovers God's standards. The sum of God's standards is comprehended in Deuteronomy 6:5 and Matthew 22:37, "Thou shalt love the Lord thy God with all thine heart, and with all they soul, and with all thy might."[10] "And what this love consists in is this: that we live and walk in accordance with and guided by His commandments (His orders, ordinances, precepts, teaching)" (2 John 6).[11]

Second, one properly applies Scripture when one realizes how far short from God's standards one has fallen.[12] The Word is a mirror that will not flatter (*cf.* James 1:23–25). When Christians do not know they are in a pit, they do not know they need to move to higher ground. Sin has a singular power to deceive, to tell us we are OK when in reality, we should "weep, mourn, and pray" (James 4:9–10) because of our sin.

Third, application occurs when there is wrought in one a love for God's standards. The Spirit actuates a hatred for all of Satan's substitutes for God's demands. The Christian, while learning to "hate every evil way," learns to love God's law—"Oh, how I love thy law!" (Ps. 119:97); "I love thy commandments above gold; yea, above fine gold" (Ps. 119:127); "I delight in the law of God after the inward man" (Rom. 7:22).[13]

Fourth, casuistry is taking place when one realizes that the Holy Spirit is the enabler to conform to God's standards. Christ, in his active obedience on earth, met the demands of the law

---

Ethics?" *The Interpretation of Scripture Today* (submitted to the RES Theological Conference, Chicago, 1984), 39.

10. Pink, 71–72.
11. The Amplified Bible.
12. Pink, 72.
13. Ibid., 75–76.

perfectly. The sole end, however, of this obedience was to render himself a perfect sacrifice to atone for the sins of his people (Heb. 2:17). By his obedience, sacrifice, and salvation of people, he secured for them the ability personally to satisfy God's demands. As Redeemer, he obtained for his people both imputed and imparted righteousness. As Procurer of the Holy Spirit, he obtained the means of imparting personal righteousness to his people. Application is the Holy Spirit's process of making Christians personally righteous. Pink elaborates:

> Christ not only rendered a perfect obedience unto the Law for the justification of His believing people, but He merited for them those supplies of the Spirit which were essential unto their sanctification, and which alone could transform carnal creatures and enable them to render acceptable obedience unto God. Though Christ died for the "ungodly" (Rom. 5:6), though He finds them ungodly (Rom. 4:5) when He justifies the ungodly, yet He does not leave them in that abominable state. On the contrary, He effectually teaches them by His Spirit to deny ungodliness and worldly lusts (Titus 2:12). Just as weight cannot be separated from a stone, or heat from a fire, so cannot justification from sanctification.[14]

Fifth, the casuistical process results in true obedience. What is true obedience to God? Obedience is not the mere external conformity to the letter of God's laws. One may have certain moral habits—integrity, punctuality, respect for others' property—yet not be spiritually obedient. True obedience is not merely conformity in an external dimension. It is "not subjection to external law"; rather, it is bequeathing authority over one's thoughts, decisions, and actions to another. Obedience is the crust of which submission to lordship is the kernel. His right is to give orders; my right is to obey orders.

Furthermore, spiritual obedience does not issue from dread of punishment. Obedience is not slavery. Neither does obedience issue from desire for rewards and favors. Obedience is not labor

---

14. Ibid., 72–73.

for wages. Neither does obedience issue from the expectation of godly peers. Obedience is not social escalation. Rather, obedience issues from heart-love. "If ye love me, keep my commandments" (John 14:23). "Spiritual and acceptable obedience ... is the heart's free response to and gratitude for the unmerited regard and love of God for us."[15]

Finally, casuistry produces spiritual prosperity. God's standards "are not grievous" (1 John 5:3) and in conforming to them "there is great reward" (Ps. 19:11). "Godliness is profitable unto all things" (1 Tim. 4:8). Applying Scripture opens the door to the path of wisdom, and wisdom's ways are "ways of pleasantness, and all her paths are peace" (Prov. 3:17). Applying Scripture allows us to "obtain the ear of God" (1 John 3:22). Applying Scripture allows God to make intimate manifestations unto the soul (John 14:21).[16] The one who delights in, meditates upon, and obeys the word will prosper in all that he does (Ps. 1:1–3). "This Book of the Law shall not depart out of your mouth, but you shall meditate on it day and night, that you may observe and do according to all that is written in it. For then you shall make your way prosperous, and then you shall deal wisely and have good success" (Josh. 1:8).[17]

CASUISTRY AND THE UNIQUENESS OF THE BIBLE

Because the Bible is a uniquely spiritual book, it must be applied through spiritual means. It is not simply like the political mandates of Chairman Mao or the rules of meditation according to the Bhagavad Gita. Only the Holy Spirit can enable the exegete to live what he sees (Rom. 8:1–4). Therefore, the means of application, the fifth element of the exegetical cycle, and consecration, the first element of the exegetical cycle, are interwoven. Application should lead to the exegete's full consecration. To know truth and not fully

---

15. Ibid., 75.
16. Ibid., 79.
17. The Amplified Bible.

obey it is not consecration. In other words, the exegetical spiral, for it to turn, requires one to apply all that has been exegeted before new exegesis is done. Application must be done before new consecration (1:1–5) can initiate a new exegesis of a passage (2:1ff.)

5.1 Perform a Casuistic Treatment upon the Text to Determine Its Uses

The term "casuistry" was in use long before the popularization of the word due to the Jesuits after the Reformation. Casuistry means to apply a principle to cases. A law student quickly learns to apply a particular statute to scenarios, so that they may learn to advise their client on ramifications. Casuistry is both the art and science of applying a principle of Scripture to every conceivable scenario. Application is comprehensive and exhaustive application.

5.2 Prepare one's heart through prayer, particularly (1) by determining personally to obey the text regardless of loss of convenience, prestige, or position, (2) by asking the Lord for wisdom not to apply the text beyond its limits or to strip the text's content, and (3) by asking the Lord for God-given care for those to whom the text applies.

Contrary to the assumption of most exegetical and homiletic procedures in print, there is no substitute for prayer. Without prayer the Bible will not be handled correctly. It will not be handled correctly in personal study or in public discourse. Prayer is essential. Do not leave your study without it.

Prayer is essential because it is the conduit through which God infuses spiritual strength. Virtually every text of Scripture, when applied, proposes some choice. Some choices cost one's comfort and/or capital; obedience to the text may cost one's power, prestige, or position. Only through prayer does the Holy Spirit infuse a believer with the spiritual strength to choose obedience.

Further, prayer is essential because the wisdom to correctly apply a text of Scripture can only come from above. Some texts may, conceivably, be overapplied. Take, for instance, "in the multitude of counselors there is safety." Does this mean that one should consult as big a multitude as possible? Should a preacher recommend his hearers to consult at least one thousand counselors before a "major" decision and at least twenty-five "minor" decisions? Should one consult twenty-five counselors for counsel on what toothpaste to buy? This text could be overapplied to the point of absurdity. Take, for instance, "let the women be clothed in modest apparel." Does this text that women must wear radiation suits at all times except when bathing, birthing, or receiving medical treatment? Spiritual wisdom keeps one from extremes; and James teaches that spiritual wisdom comes from above. But prayer is also essential is to keep from underapplying the text. "Cutting off the rough edges" of a text to render it palatable to a spiritually immature congregation is clergy malpractice.

Finally, prayer is essential for the development of sincere compassion for those to whom the text applies. Love without truth is "wishy-washy"; truth without love is either Phariseeism or bitterness. True preaching counsels people to change out of heartfelt compassion. Love must propel what the preacher tells others to do. And, no hearer should ever leave a sermon without some sense of what the text instructs the hearer to do.

5.3 Brainstorm: List every conceivable scenario to which the text may apply. The "cases" to which the text may apply is casuistry. Then list corresponding questions about how the text would change each scenario. The changes to each case are the "uses" of the text.

Consider, for instance, the command of Paul: "A women should learn in quietness and full submission. I do not permit a woman to teach or to have authority over a man; she must be silent. For Adam was formed first, then Eve. And Adam was not the one deceived; it was the woman who was deceived and became a sinner"

(1 Tim. 2:11–14). A casuistical treatment of this text would explore the following cases:

> Is Paul speaking from culture, or from Christ?
>
> Is the injunction only relevant to where the gift of tongues was abused in Paul's day?
>
> Should a woman ever teach a man the Bible?
>
> Should a woman ever teach a man anything?
>
> Should a godly woman ever teach an unsaved man the Bible?
>
> Is this injunction limited?
>
> Does it apply only to the 11:00 Sunday morning service?
>
> Does it apply to Sunday school?
>
> Does this apply only to services on the Sabbath or the Lord's day?
>
> Does it apply to Christian schools, including colleges and seminaries?
>
> Can a woman teach men if her father or husband, who would be her "head," is present?
>
> Can a woman pray in public?
>
> What about the women who prophesied in the Old Testament and Acts (*cf.* 21:9)?
>
> Can a women write a commentary on the Bible?
>
> Can she give "testimonies" in worship services?
>
> Can she read the Scripture in public?
>
> Can she give prayer requests in a service?
>
> Can she sing in a service?
>
> What about family worship at home; can she teach there?
>
> Can she teach young children? When are children too old for this?

FIFTH PHASE

5.4 Verify That Each Change Would Not Violate the Analogy of Scripture

These questions relevant to a casuistical treatment illustrate the necessity of enlargement before casuistry. Any portion of Scripture must be interpreted in light of the analogy of the whole Bible in order for it to be applied accurately. For instance, this text would have to be enlarged according 1 Corinthians 11:2–16, 14:34–35, and Titus 2:3–5, in order to exegete answers to the questions above. Casuistry is simply taking a text, enlarging it according to Puritan principles, and relating it to every conceivable scenario relevant to it.

5.5 Compare One's Own "Uses" with the "Uses" in the Puritan Commentaries and Add to or Refine One's List Accordingly

Puritan commentaries follow the pattern of their sermons—exposition, doctrine, and application. The applicatory section, or the text's "uses," are directly valuable to this point of the exegetical process. The best Puritan commentaries for each book of the Bible were listed in the section called "Fourth Phase: Enlargement into Doctrine."

5.6 Each "Use" Is a Preaching Point. Develop Each Preaching Point through the Rhetorical Processes

Each "use" of the text derived in "5" should be expressed in a complete sentence. A preaching point ought to be a complete sentence for the sake of clarity. The "use" preaching points can be developed rhetorically through the four rhetorical processes: explanation, illustration, argumentation, and exhortation.

Conclusion: "Pulling It All Together" into a Sermon

    A. Take the homiletic outline developed in 2.2e and pray over each point.

1. Pray over the text's thesis first.
2. Pray over the text's preaching points next.

B. Weave the preaching points taken from other steps into the homiletic outline.

C. Develop the preaching points.

1. Seek illustrations for preaching points; answer "What does this point look like?"
2. Develop explanations for preaching points; answer "What does this point mean?"
3. Devise arguments for preaching points; answer "Why should I believe or obey this point?"
4. Draw up exhortations for preaching points; answer "What encouragements are there for me to believe or obey this point?"
5. Use applications of preaching points; answer "How will this point change my life and the lives of others?"

D. Organize the preaching points logically.

E. Rehearse the sermon as many times as necessary.

F. "Preach the Word!" (2 Tim. 4:2).

BIBLIOGRAPHY

Baron, David. *Types, Psalms, and Prophecies*. Minneapolis: Klock & Klock, 1907.
Childs, Brevard S. *Biblical Theology in Crisis*. Philadelphia: Westminster, 1970.
Davidson, Richard M. *Typology in Scripture*. Berrien Springs, Mich.: Andrews University Press, 1981.
Denten, Robert C. *A First Reader in Biblical Theology*. New York: Seabury, 1961.
Diel, Paul. *Symbolism in The Bible*. San Francisco: Harper & Row, 1986.
Fairbairn, Patrick. *Typology of Scripture*. Grand Rapids: Kregel, 1989.
Foulkes, Francis. *The Acts of God*. London: Tyndale, 1955.
Geisler, Norman. *To Understand the Bible Look for Jesus*. Grand Rapids: Baker, 1968.
Gese, Hartmut. *Essays on Biblical Theology*. Minneapolis: Augsburg, 1981.
Goppelt, Leonhard. *Typos: The Typological Interpretation of the Old Testament in the New*. Grand Rapids: Eerdmans, 1982.
Green, James Benjamin. *A Harmony of the Westminster Presbyterian Standards*. Collins World, 1976.
Harrington, Wilfrid J. *The Path of Biblical Theology*. Dublin: Gil and Macmillan, 1973.
Keach, Benjamin. *Preaching from the Types and Metaphors of the Bible*. Grand Rapids: Kregel, 1972
Lampe, G.W.H., and Woollcombe, K.J. *Essays on Typology*. Naperville, Ill.: Allenson, 1957.
Lawton, Steward. *Pastoral Implications of Biblical Theology*. New York: Seabury, 1968.
Lowance, Mason Ira, Jr. "Images and Shadows of Divine Things: Puritan Typology in New England from 1660 to 1750." Ph.D. dissertation, Graduate School of Emory University, 1967.
March, W. Eugene, ed. *Texts and Testaments: Critical Essays on the Bible and Early Church Fathers*. San Antonio: Trinity University, 1980.
Mather, Samuel. *The Gospel of the Old Testament*. London: Seeley and Burnside, 1834.

BIBLIOGRAPHY

McCurley, Foster R., and John Reumann. *Witness of the Word*. Philadelphia: Fortress, 1986.

M'Ewen, William. *Grace and Truth; or the Glory and Fulness of the Redeemer Displayed: In an Attempt to Illustrate and Enforce the Most Remarkable Types, Figures and Allegories of the Old Testament*. London: Hamilton, Adams, 1841.

Payne, J. Barton. *The Theology of the Older Testament*. Grand Rapids: Academie, 1962.

Pipa, John A., Jr. "William Perkins and the Development of Puritan Preaching." Ph.D. thesis, Westminster Theological Seminary, 1985.

Prickett, Stephen. *Words and The Word*. Cambridge: Cambridge University Press, 1986.

Schuyleman. *Symbolisms of the Bible*. Boston: Meador, 1942.

Vos, Geerhardus. *Biblical Theology: Old and New Testaments*. Grand Rapids: Eerdmans, 1948.

Wenham, John W. *Christ and The Bible*. Downers Grove, Ill.: InterVarsity, 1972.

Wood, Charles M. *The Formation of Christian Understanding*. Philadelphia: Westminster, 1981.

www.ingramcontent.com/pod-product-compliance
Lightning Source LLC
Chambersburg PA
CBHW062043220426
43662CB00010B/1625